PEACEFUL MILES

10 Spiritual Paths of Success in Sports and Life.

Based on real facts

RICARDO SALA

Translation by Claudia Valdez

Peaceful Miles   Ricardo Sala

Dedications

Dedicated to all those people who are open to experience life and sports in a different way to obtain high doses of pleasant spiritual abundance.

To my whole genealogical family tree, regardless if they are present or if they have already left.

To my father, because without him and his teachings I would not live life like I do now.

To my mother, who is the pillar of the order that governs my life.

To my brothers, who along with my parents, were the first people I met, with whom I lived, played, slept, argued and embraced in my life.

To my life partner and my two wonderful children who are the driving force of my days.

To my friends, with whom I've been united with since we became friends.

To my colleagues and friends from college, with admiration and gratitude for giving me so much from desk times to present.

To all, with love.

Contents

Meet the Author

Ricardo Sala was born in the city of Saltillo, Coahuila, in Mexico. He studied law in the city of Monterrey, Mexico, and Neurosciences in London, England. He has a PhD by the Universidad Complutense of Madrid. He has a Master's Degree in Administration from Saint Mary's University in San Antonio, Texas in the United States. He has a specialty in International Relations by Harvard University, at Cambridge.

He is currently a business, mental and spiritual coach, applied to business and sports organizations.

He is the only Mexican in the world certified to teach Neuro-Linguistic Programming courses and workshops endorsed by the International Trainers Association of London.

He is a mental and spiritual coach for professional teams and individual athletes. From professionals or Olympians, to amateurs and recreational.

He is a neuroscientific program designer for human development in companies and private organizations.

He lectures and writes human and spiritual development books.

Professor in college majors, masters and doctorates in different universities in northern Mexico.

He is currently an active ultra-distance athlete.

He has represented Mexico in sports in national, international and world competitions. Some of his most significant ultra-distance sports achievements are:

- EVEREST TRAIL RACE. 260K running (Nepal and Himalayas).
- TORRES DE PAINE ULTRA TRAIL. 80K running (Chilean Patagonia).

- (LA RUTA DE LOS CONQUISTADORES) THE ROUTE OF THE CONQUERORS. 260K in MTB (Costa Rica).
- TITAN DESERT RACE. 668K in MTB (Sahara Desert, Morocco).
- ULTRA TRAIL DU MONT BLANC. 101K running. (Switzerland, France and Italy).
- ULTRAMAN 520K triathlon. (Penticton, B.C., Canada).
- 13x IRONMAN.

Additionally, he has finished countless marathons, triathlons and duathlons, as well as Ultra Distance trail races in Mexico of 80K or more.

He has traveled the Way of Saint James by bicycle and running, completing the route's 801K.

In his trips, both to study and to compete, he has stayed in Buddhist monasteries in Nepal and Tibet, learning their philosophy and their spiritual resources for life, which he practices and teaches in the West.

* *Special Note:* The present summary of studies and facts about the author was presented with no intention of leading the reader to believe that this is what defines him as a person or even to show off. The intention is just to let you know the type of activities he practices and his lifestyle.

Foreword

If the word "genuine" had a person in whom to represent it, it would be Ricardo Sala. Those of us who know him know that everything for him is freedom. Freedom to think, to do, to blend styles, to experiment. He very much acts in a "lets-se-what-happens-if..." way, and he does it so that he can experiment everything on his own, rather than someone telling him about it. He seeks results, let them come, sometimes favorable and others unfavorable, but always learns with experience. And precisely this book is the result of experiments that he discovered within himself, and that, without any doubt for him, favor human beings. To get to write what he wrote, he first had to make sure it was real. This is just the way he is, and this is how his lifestyle works.

This book represents that perfect fusion between a warrior who fights life in an all-out war, but with spiritual tools. I found that spectacular and especially, genuine. Finding the fusion of a person who competes giving all he has, leaving his heart in every step he takes, but without anyone really knowing that in his interior he is kind of a calm Buddhist monk. One of those you can only find in movies. Ricardo practices his life philosophy every day. If you talk to him or watch some of his videos on social media, you will notice that he speaks with such passion and strength that he electrifies you. However, his words are profound, as well as his metaphorical phrases. You would never expect that amid so much dynamism, so much intensity, you can suddenly find yourself with spiritual advice or a personal phrase that will leave you thinking that life has also another side, another focus and another color. Ricardo simply takes you out of your own mind. You just have to listen to him, or in this case, read him.

The author lives convinced of his lifestyle and its enormous benefits. Perhaps that is why he needs to share them in a simple and helpful way. He explains his perception of the world as a reality that can be altered at will. While it is difficult to change what is outside of us, he mentions how we can change it within ourselves, the way we wish to do so. *"Peaceful Miles"* is that, a change of world. A change that is real. A change of life from the most important place for each one of us: from within. Mind and heart.

The different paths of the book will make us reflect and put ourselves into action for our own good. Ricardo reflects and insists at all times on the benefits of each spiritual law that he practices and writes for us in this work. He invites us, and at the same time challenges us, to examine a place that is little visited for fear of finding something that we do not like: our interior. He challenges us to self-knowledge, and once we are in there, he takes us to come face to face with our ego in order to understand and master it. Taming of the ego, as he calls it, is perhaps the most difficult and oldest challenge human beings have ever had in history. Ricardo makes us face it and become aware of the importance of knowing it, so we can deprive ourselves of its intentions and be able to move forward, but now with a perspective full of peace.

Ricardo shows us with diligence, discipline and dedication, the paths, ways, laws, trails, experiences and warriors that appear in this real-life adventure called reading *"Peaceful Miles."*

His words awaken things that motivate us to live and embark on a journey into ourselves. The Zen warrior who appears in his chapters is only himself turned into a character who pretends to appear to be an unreal being, however, he is real. The proof is that his name is Ricardo Sala. He practices humbleness so much that he preferred to create a fictional being to speak on his behalf. When you read anecdotes about the Zen warrior, it is the author himself, that is how he is in real life, and that is why we will have to learn from him through this work, which must be put into practice. He mentions that we all have a warrior of light that lives within each of us. We will just have to train him to know what we are capable of. If you decide to practice what is cited in this book, you will reach the summit of your own existence.

Anonymous

16

Introduction

This journey, embodied in words, was born with the intention of sharing the spiritual resources that changed my life when I began to practice them, and which became part of my personal and sporting lifestyle, giving it a sense of abundance without shortages or lack of peace. The paths or spiritual laws that I describe taught me to think big, without the need to have things, desired results, prizes, medals or trophies.

I write this book with the permission given to me by the experience of living in a material world for years, thinking that what you have is above what you are.

I write with the same permission given by competing in life and in sports for years with the goal of winning at all costs, stepping all over myself, without even realizing what I was becoming.

I write with the permission given by having been in those emotional places in which I thought that life was like that, believing that my achievements and success would define me as a person.

I have enjoyed the ephemeral pleasure of a victory or a personal success, realizing that it is really like a nice fresh fog: it does not allow you to see the immensity of the spectacular and beautiful landscape lying on the background.

Now, I live and compete with an abundant sense of peace, serenity, love, compassion and happiness. I would never go back to my old practices about the material world. Having tried the abundance of the spiritual world, it would be illogical to go back. There is no comparison between these two worlds.

I would like to comment that, if today's Ricardo Sala met with himself from a few years ago, he would hardly recognize him. It is with that permission that I write this book, because I know what it is like to be in both places: in the struggle without purpose of the material environment, and to be at peace in the spiritual universe, training to be a sort of peaceful warrior.

In this book, we will travel together ten spiritual paths or laws. By practicing them you will be able to experience an abundance that you would have never imagined.

We will start the journey with the *Path of Purpose*, which will give you an idea of what life and sports are all about in the spiritual world. After, we will travel the roads of *Taming the Ego* and personal *Self-control*, which we need to start acting in other more pleasant ways. Later, we will be on the path of the much sought-after way of living in the present *Here and Now*. You will find practical ways to achieve it. The *Path of Potentiality or Karma* will also be traveled, with high doses of reflection about your daily actions. It will explain to you in a very simple way how this law works. Halfway through the trip, we will be taking the *Path of Fluency*, explaining the behavior of nature and the universe, becoming aware that we are part of it, and how we can act in the same way without unnecessary efforts. Well into the spiritual path of the book, we will find the laws of *Humbleness, Detachment and Acceptance.* Laws or paths that are extremely necessary to transcend within ourselves and subsequently transcend outside. We will intentionally finish with the *Path of Happiness*. There, we can combine all the paths that converge in the enormous path of spiritual serenity.

You will find fables and metaphors of the Zen warrior continously. A fiction character whom I identify with and constantly seizes me during my life. He will be our teacher and spiritual guide. He will take us to a world of imagination and motivation because of his perspective of life and its situations.

I invite you to open your mind and heart. I invite you to take your own spiritual path with this instruction manual that will lead you to experience things with your body, mind and soul in ways you would have never imagined. If you are an athlete, I invite you to challenge yourself to leave your current competition practices and start a personal spiritual leadership to transcend as a human being. If you are not an athlete, there is also a challenge that you can face, by waking up and transcending in your daily lifestyle.

I warn you: this book is not science fiction. Nor is it something unattainable or utopian. This book talks about real laws for the spirit that apply in a real, current world and that evolve your being in a real way. You just have to practice and practice so that you can live and experience its sublime effects.

Everything you will read works and has worked in my life for years. That is why I dare to share everything here. They are tools that I use daily and that are part of my personal style and way of being. The more you practice them, the more skillful and expert you will become to apply them. However, never believe that you have mastered them perfectly, since there is always more to learn from them as you use them more.

I invite you to evolve, so we can transcend as human beings and as athletes. In that strict order. I invite you to this trip of ten paths that will make you see and feel things differently. In a way of abundant satisfaction and happiness.

Welcome to this trip. Here we go.

Ricardo Sala.

CHAPTER 1

Path of Purpose

«Whether you win or lose is not what is important. What is important is what you become when you win or lose.»

- Ricardo Sala.

What is your purpose in life? What is the true purpose of playing sports? These are two frequently asked questions that the spiritual path answers with acute certainty. However, and as with all paths captured here, you must walk on that trail in order to truly enjoy the Law of Purpose. You must walk day and night, with rain or sun, with cold or heat, at all times regardless of circumstances.

I intentionally decided to start this book's journey with the Path of Purpose. The intention is first to answer some questions that are necessary for this spiritual adventure. Questions like: Why undertake this trip? Why read this book? Why practice sports? What is the purpose of living?

This is the starting point. We will have to identify the purpose of what we do, otherwise, most things would not make sense.

Why do we set a goal? Why do we get up every morning to do what we do? Why do we want what we want?

Not knowing the answers to all the previous questions would be like walking or running through life without a compass.

In the field of sports, the purpose will never be to win or to be a better athlete, let alone be better than another person. Never.

That goal is very limited, material and ephemeral, it should not be even considered as a purpose. There would be little or no transcendence. How long does a compliment last? How long does the memory of a medal last? Or that of a trophy? Very little, compared to what we can do in sports to develop as a person, inspiring, motivating and transcending personally to leave permanent and eternal legacies.

Nor does the Path of Purpose refers to the typical phrase: *"To win is not what is most important, but to have fun is."* Of course, fun should be a part of life and sports, and it would be an attitude that adds up, however, the Law of Purpose does not refer only to fun. That attitude is positive if a purpose exists, since having fun is not a spiritual purpose but an accessory, a useful ingredient, but it could not survive on its own if it is not attached to the purpose.

Purpose is not the same as intention or objective. Objectives are the goals that you set for achieving them. Your intention to practice sports might be to keep you in optimal physical shape, lose weight, make friends, have a healthy life, etc. However, neither your goals or objectives, nor your intention is close to the true purpose.

I always suggest to people that their sports goals or objectives shall have nothing to do with ego issues. That they shouldn't want to win to prove something, not even to themselves. In short: that their goals shall have nothing to do with believing that they will define them as persons.

We must first distinguish between personal purpose and sports purpose. The sports part refers to the technique, the body, the muscular and physical performance, to a certain skill that increases with training. In the personal level, it means your development as a human being, in the values that you are training, in humbleness, in what you sow in others, in a few words: in what you become as a person when practicing sports. It is to leave eternal legacies with your actions, with the example and everything that has to do with the development of your being.

The result you have should serve only to increase the wisdom of your mind and spirit, and not to believe that you need special treatment or making you believe that you are a better person. The result of a competition does not define you as a person. If you win, it means that you are good for that sport at that time, but it does not mean that you are good in all other aspects of your life, which are the ones that really matter.

If your successes, achievements, triumphs, social position, or awards do not define you as a person or tell you who you are, then what does define you? You are defined by your actions towards others. As simple as that. You are really that, regardless of whether you are "successful" or not, your way of being is what you really are and what defines you.

I practice two types of purposes, although in reality there is only one, but let's say I split it in two. I call one of those purposes *earthly* and the other, *spiritual*. The earthly purpose is to set an example, the spiritual purpose is being, giving and serving.

EARTHLY PURPOSE

The purpose which I call *earthly* means that I practice sports with the sole intention of being an example to others that everything is possible. It is to motivate, to share different ways of thinking. In the end, what I am looking for is to persuade and challenge people to live their sport and their lives in a spiritual way, but at the same time showing them that sports and their own life in its material form have limitations. I am looking to make people think. Think of different, not established things. One of them and the main one, is that they enter an event or competition and live it spiritually, with another sense that is much more beneficial, satisfying, pure, beautiful and lasting.

Every time I wake up, every morning I get up and train, it is with only one purpose: to be an example with my actions, to inspire others and live our own moments. Starting with my family. With such a purpose, how can I not wake up with energy ? What else can I need or ask for?

A secondary gain from practicing sports is that I am training for essential things in life. If you don't practice sports it doesn't matter, living without practicing sports is also like a sport. Sport teaches me to be disciplined, to face adversities, to manage my time, to win and lose, to compete healthily and without ego, to set goals, to execute plans, to see how I achieve something based on facts, or how I manage not to see them if I do not act, to love, to cry without sorrow, to care for others, to give. Sports nourishes the person more than the body. What you learn by practicing sports lasts for a lifetime. Achievements and awards only last a certain time. In fact, very little. The rest is lasting.

The earthly purpose is to leave legacies. And, what is a legacy? A legacy means that your actions today benefit someone else in the future, whether or not you are present, whether you are alive or dead. It is planting a tree today so that it will give shade to someone else tomorrow, even if you don't even know the people who will benefit from your actions today.

The purpose will always be what I become during the time I practice sports. If you practice sports spiritually, you will live a spiritual life. When living a spiritual life, you will live awake and enjoy states of love, joy, happiness and permanent peace within. There, you experience personal enlightenment.

Don't let the world of competing against another or against yourself take over your purposes as a person. Think about your loved ones, your children, your parents, your friends all over the world and leave examples to them through sports.

SPIRITUAL PURPOSE

The purpose which I call *spiritual*, is the true and only purpose of life: TO LIVE.

Goals should never be your purposes. A person without purpose focuses on their challenges, their achievements or their talents.

Personal goals and achievements are very small and limited. Personal success is about yourself, instead, adding meaning to the lives of others with the acts you practice is priceless and infinite. The priority of your actions and challenges should be focused on what happens to and counts for other people. Your life must make a difference for others and not just for yourself.

How to achieve that? Very simple: put others before yourself. Serve others. To serve is to put others before yourself. It seems that life is only about ourselves, and it is true, but that is only the first step, since what transcends and the true purpose is that your actions sow something in the lives of others. It is your life sown in other people. It is pouring yourself onto others. We impact through legacy. The purpose is to live adding value to the lives of others using your strengths.

Comments like "' I'm doing an ironman in a couple of months,' ' I qualified for a world cup,' ' This brand is sponsoring me,' ' I'll be the best,' ' I was born to run,' ' I'm made for extreme challenges,' ' I want to be number one,' ' I want to break my own record,'" are several of the examples that you can listen to or tell yourself if you only live with personal goals, with ego, and obviously without a spiritual purpose. All of the above will come or not, but that does not matter. If it comes it is a consequence of something you did and you will be happy for a moment, but your chances of achieving your goal will increase if you have the true purpose: the spiritual one.

A person without purpose will believe that their purpose is every challenge, thing, event or project that they are set out to accomplish in their life. For those who don't know where they want to go, it seems any train can take them. The end is never the purpose, since the end would not be in the present, it would be in the imaginary creation of something you call future. Nor will the finish line of a race be in the present, unless you are crossing it at that precise moment.

For example, while writing this book I don't think about its end. My purpose is just to write, and I focus on it. I capture what I am writing here and now in this moment. That's how I do everything in my life as a purpose. As we mentioned, to live adding meaning to the lives of others is the real purpose.

Explained in another way, and quoting the spiritual master Osho, it is not the same to play than to play a game. Running is not the same as running in a competition. When running at an event, if you think about the result you want, you lose your purpose in that moment. The purpose is to run with everything there is within you, with everything that makes you listen, see what surrounds you in detail and feel your whole body, without thinking about the result. The key is to compete without expectations and thus feel the true purpose of life, not to mention how light and peacefully you will compete.

There is a big difference between playing and playing a game. The game has a purpose: to win. In the game you have to be attentive to the result. A victory to be achieved. The opponent must be defeated. If you play like that, then playing becomes a game and that is when you lose your purpose. The activity of playing is enough on its own, don't look any further, however, we want so eagerly to achieve the triumph or the goal we forget to live.

When you simply play there is no added goal or another objective, just to play. Life is playing, and sports are a part of life, not life itself.

The moment you decide to just play, you will be ready to enlighten yourself and feel the magic of the spiritual world. There, in that place, you will be really living and you will feel that you are in another dimension.

On the other hand, if your goal or achievement is your purpose, when you get it you will have to find another purpose and then another purpose, then another, and so on, and so will your life go by. Stop the wheel of goals and focus on living. With objectives, but without missing the present. Distinguishing between both concepts.

From the world in general, some want money, power, prestige, things, awards, praise and, then what? If that is your state of purpose, even getting all that, you lose anyway. Even if you win or get your wish, over time you will realize that there is a new void that will have to be filled and you will want something else. You will start playing new games and again your mind will fall into that state of permanent deception. A new world of desires will open and you will enter again into the wheel-with-no-end of chasing, instead of just running. The purpose is only to play without beginnings or endings. Just playing, with your mind set on adding wonderful things to other people.

Run, don't chase. Run without imagining destiny or goal, just run. What is within you is what is valuable, it is your own energy connected with yourself to achieve unimaginable performance. Stop collecting information from the outside, that is just a mental creation, your fantasy, your own inventions. There is nothing outside of you, you do not exist as yourself, so don't live as if the outside were the world you need to have an abundant physical and spiritual performance in sports or in life.

When you discover that no goal is the real purpose, that no goal is really useful for your performance and development, then that's when you find the nothing-to-do state, you just have to BE.

What is sought is to play without playing games. To play without playing games you must be in the strict present feeling every muscle, feeling every drop of sweat, both when you compete and when you train. Feel everything. From when you sign up for a challenge all the way to when you cross the finish line, but with your senses sharpened every moment, in the present. That is living.

Flora, fauna and all nature have no goals or objectives, that is why it is so beautiful and perfect. Its purpose is as ours should be, just to live.

When you forget the finish line, when you forget the stopwatch that marks the time you have to break, when you forget the triumph you must achieve, in that moment your limits vanish. That is when you manage to find and experience your maximum potential, both physical and mental. Relax your mind and you will feel the tension disappear. Keep only your exclusive purity. Live moment by moment, step by step, yard by yard, point by point, execution by execution, as if the future did not exist. In this way you will achieve the sublime: you will become the purpose.

Perhaps too many goals have ruled your life. Now, give yourself the fantastic opportunity to govern yourself living moment by moment as if the future did not exist. In the beginning of your spiritual training *"pretending there is no future"* will be conscious and you will feel something that you were not used to thinking and feeling, as if it is being forced upon you. It is normal. However, with time and practice it will become a natural state and you will do it as it really is, without a future.

Find the beautiful purpose of not having success in your mind. Do not become a slave of desires or get caught in them. When you live the true purpose of every spiritual athlete, you will already be what you were looking for or pursuing with such longing: the satisfaction of being your true BEING. That is the only reality and purpose. Live and add meaning to the world.

HOW TO ACHIEVE THE PATH OF PURPOSE

1. Put others before yourself.
2. Develop appreciation for others with your actions.
3. Change yourself and your priorities, before wishing to change other people.
4. Add value to others using your strengths.
5. Execute the activity or sport you practice as if the future did not exist. If you are playing sports such as tennis or golf, stop thinking about the result you

imagine during the performance. Just let it be and focus 100% on the present.

6. In sports like running, cycling or triathlon, stop thinking about the clock, the finish line and everything you prepared, as if it did not exist, as if it were a fantasy, an invention that you know never existed. Train and compete without a future.

7. Compete without judging your performances or results. Keep your own prejudices away. Do not grade yourself or compare yourself with anyone else.

8. Enclose yourself in a kind of peaceful sphere, where the world may be burning outside, but inside, you are like the depth of the sea, calm.

9. Every time you train or compete, let it be without expectations.

10. Sharpen your senses to the extent of just feeling the moment.

11. Always ask yourself the question: What am I becoming?

    Ask yourself this constantly while you practice your sport or while performing any activity in your life. Whichever. This will allow you to know where you're at and know where you're going to, which will give you an idea of your outcome as a person.

Practice these forms as much as necessary until you achieve the ease that your body, mind and soul need. The same ease found within the energy of the universe.

CHAPTER 2

Path of Taming the Ego

«Like a rose that lives in harmony with its thorns without them hurting it, so the ego lives within ourselves.»

- Ricardo Sala.

First, I would like to define what is understood as ego.

From a collection of definitions, mainly from literature, the ego is defined as the thought that makes us feel superior to other people or even superior to nature. It is an excessive overvaluation of oneself. It is that state of the "I" that makes us believe that we have a special capacity over other things and people. It is the "I" before "US" or "THEY."

Let's say that said definition is correct, at least in theory, however, it is incomplete.

How could we complement it and make it more truthful?

The ego, in addition to the previous definition, is also:

1) What other people can think about me regarding my actions.
2) What other people can say about me regarding my actions.
3) The need for people's approval regarding my actions.

It is very important to establish that the ego feeds on FEAR. A person without a tamed ego is scared to death every day and at all times if their actions are not approved by society. *"What will they say"* and *"what will they think of me"* are a constant fear that keeps us away from our being and essence, even from our will to do something or act in some way. Ego is a social mask that disguises our being and that is worn so that other people's approval is risked the least possible.

Fear is a thought created by our mind that triggers chemical substances that make us take actions in the present based on experiences from the past or creations from the future. What ego actually fears is not being accepted, being rejected, or not to belong to a certain group to which the person believes belonging to will define him or her as a person. The ego is like a fierce animal that lives inside us that feeds on the achievements we have to believe that we are happy.

I would like to be very intentional in explaining that having a tamed ego does not mean that you don't care what people think or say about you. It matters, but it does not modify your being. It matters in a compassionate spiritual way. It matters to transcend in others, not to feed your apparent value over others. Giving without expecting to receive something in return is a beautiful way to keep the ego away. If we don't need even the gratitude of those who we give to or serve, that is really giving. Expecting something in return would already be sort of a contract with rights and obligations for both parties. If when you give something you expect something in return, it is the ego that asks for it, because it wants recognition for your actions. Let us not allow it to interfere in a wonderful process such as giving and serving others. The ego is scared to death because of its unhealthy need for approval. It is not that our own approval or satisfaction with our actions are not enough for it, rather than that, it doesn't even see or feel them.

The ego is linked to the Path of Self-control (Chapter 3) which mentions that said ego believes that our achievements define us as persons. If so, what would happen if success disappears? What would happen if you no longer have the position you had in your job? What would happen if you are no longer the number one of your sport? Would you disappear? Would your essence or person disappear? Obviously not. You would be left with your real and pure being. But if you did not meet frequently with it during your life, the reunion with your being will be more complex. There are even humans who never met with their being again because they thought that in life they were their social position, and they believed that that was what defined them as human beings. Sadly, there are people who die without ever connecting, or only sporadically, with their being.

Another characteristic of the ego is that it is nosy. It wants to have the leading role. It wants to enter and be part of every day-to-day activity and it does it through our thoughts to later, if you allow it, become your actions. It does it out of the fear of wanting to support itself from people and from the outside, since its interior is empty.

Just as the body can be trained, so, identically, the ego is trained. Just like a fierce animal that you want to tame, the ego is also tamed by working and training it daily throughout our lives. Even the oldest Buddhist monks continue to train their ego daily, since keeping the ego still and quiet is a task that has no end. Therefore, I define such training of the ego as a way of life, rather than a task that starts and ends.

You will always have to be aware of the ego and how it can influence your decisions. Decisions that initially seem harmless, but over time can drift you away from the real purpose of living.

COMPETING WITH EGO

Ever since my childhood, until a few years ago, I competed and trained with ego. I know perfectly what it is like to be there. However, to some extent, I think it is a natural process. The problem is when you continue to compete with ego over time and never worry about training it for it to appear more and more tamed in your life, obviously including your sporting life.

When I competed with ego I didn't realize that I competed like that. I thought it was normal that I always wanted to win over others, wanting to finish before others, wanting to improve whatever personal time, or going for a medal to hang it somewhere for others to see my achievement. Even uploading my achievements to my social media without the purpose of adding meaning to the lives of others. I thought it was all about winning and improving as an athlete, regardless that I was trampling over myself.

Despite having received a good education with values and learning not to practice hatred and resentment, when I competed with ego, I made two or three good enemies. And all that for wanting to prove that I was better than them, or that what they said or thought of me was not true. So, I defended myself when I should have really kept silent and looked inside. Ego kept me from seeing that what you achieve doesn't matter, but rather what matters is how you are in your actions. The importance of the place where you arrive at shouldn't really be a priority, but what you become as a person when you arrive. I have seen people leave the competition when they realize that their result will not be what they wanted or what their ego was looking for. They quit inventing an excuse they can show to society and thus, their ego justifies their abandonment, but at the same time they are interrupting their spiritual growth and the great experience of not achieving what the ego desires.

Comments like "'I have a bad stomachache, something made me sick and I had to abandon,' 'I couldn't stand my knee so I withdrew from the competition,' 'I came in twentieth because I had a mechanical problem with my bike.'"

Comments and justifications of that kind are more than common in the world of sports. Even if those explanations have been real, when your ego is tamed, it is not necessary to explain anything. You just declare the result, that's all. We give an explanation because we need to be justified before the outside world in order to feel less bad.

Competing with ego is a fairly heavy and hard task. You carry the approval you need from people to be "happy" or calm. You live and compete for others, instead of fully living your own experience.

COMPETING WITHOUT EGO

Over time, after understanding the intentions and the way of acting of the ego, I began to tame it little by little. Without my intrusive ego in my life, I gave myself the wonderful opportunity to experience situations unthinkable for me when the results mattered to me. I started to compete sometimes giving less than my ability, letting other competitors defeat me, who would normally not do so. At first, my ego reproached me and told me that I could not allow that person to pass me or win, tempting me to give it all. However, it was not about the result, but about my own spiritual training that I had decided to carry out. At that time it was not about my physical or mental capacity, but about my spiritual training.

I repeated and repeated the formula of competing regardless of the outcome or if someone else beat me. People even spoke about my poor sports performance; however, I knew that the need to speak and defend myself was the one that should also be trained and kept out. Always aware that I no longer needed social masks.

I was literally freeing myself from all the opinions and approvals from the outside world. I kept calm, quiet and even praising the capabilities of the rest of my competition partners. My "food" to achieve this was a phrase that settled in my mind, which I always repeated when I was tempted to speak or defend myself:

«No success or failure defines me.»

Competing without ego took away all the pressure I previously had when competing. My fears vanished and a world without limits opened before me.

My personal and professional life began to be fulfilling and calm. I stopped bragging about personal comments or comments on social media about how *"good"* I was. I stopped giving that sense of recognition or prominence when I posted something or uploaded a picture to my media. Currently, everything I post is for the sole purpose of motivating, setting an example and adding meaning to the lives of others, always emphasizing that the result is completely irrelevant compared to what you become when it happens (whatever the result). The first thing I think about when posting something onto my social media is how to add value to someone else with what I upload. I think of them first, instead of me. If I can't find something that adds to someone else, I simply don't upload it. I do the same when I appear in public.

Keeping the ego out of the way, as a simple spectator, I began this stage of immense peace in which I stopped suffering when there were some negative comments from the people, just as I stopped boasting when there were flattering comments. I knew that my own being was what counted for my experiences.

When competing with ego, you avoid living experiences where you really find all the happiness, peace and love abundantly. When you live and compete without ego, it makes you think that you would never like to live again as before. There is so much abundance in this spiritual path that wishing to return to ancient practices would be unthinkable. When your ego has been tamed, you can be in a race or game and you don't feel anything negative. You don't feel anything because you are so immersed in your abundant peace that you do not notice those things that were apparently important, but which actually are banalities compared to your being. In this way, everything is very nice. You give your best in body, mind and soul, always being very intentional as to the thought that the result will not define you as a person.

After I began practicing having my being above the ego, on one occasion I finished a competition, and a person against whom I competed approached me and said:

> — "You won Ricardo! You're the best! Congratulations!" - and gave me a strong high-five.

— "Thank you!" - I thanked him from my heart - "I am not the best, friend, it's only that today I won. Next time it can be you or someone else." - I replied calmly with another high-five.

In the same competition I unintentionally heard that another person commented:

- "Ricardo Sala won, it bothers me that he wins."

I smiled inside, I was silent, without the slightest temptation to think of something that disturbed my serenity. His comment was diluted in my peace of mind. His comment referred to a result and my being was intact.

HOW TO ACHIEVE THE PATH OF TAMING THE EGO

1. Be aware of your ego. If you do not realize that it is present meddling, you cannot begin to tame it.
2. Be intentionally humble.

3. Think that what you do does not define you as a person. Only your way of being and attitude define you.

4. Realize that the ego will always want to defend itself or boast about a comment from someone else.

5. Give yourself the opportunity to practice taming the ego by remaining silent when you are tempted to say something important about yourself or defend yourself. The ego loves to talk, especially about itself.

6. Stop talking about your achievements. Talk about your experiences without saying what your results were, with the sole intention of adding in people with what you say.

7. Identify if someone else is sharing something with you, and you think of yourself, move that thought away by being aware that at that moment it is not about yourself, but about the other person.

CHAPTER 3

Path of Self-control

«Not even your most bitter rival will hurt you as much as your own negative thoughts.»

- Ricardo Sala.

Being under control means owning the movements of your mind, soul and body. To have internal control is to be intelligent in all aspects. Your decisions will have the smallest range for mistakes and your state will be that of inner peace.

The Path of Internal Self-control is to have emotional control of yourself at all times. Only each one of us has the decision and the absolute power to control our emotions.

Emotions sometimes come without us having full will, they are like the weather, they arrive because of the moment that a person or athlete lives and experiences at that precise moment. However, the emotion as such is not the one that could make you lose control, but rather the lack of awareness and control of it.

In order to control an emotion it is necessary to realize that it is present. That way you own the feeling and not vice versa. If the emotion controls you because you don't realize you are experimenting it, at that moment you are at the mercy of its effects and consequences.

The Path of Self-control has to do with emotional intelligence. It is about being intelligent when thoughts that could enhance or diminish the performance and execution of the activity appear. Any thought that does not add up must be cut at the root, as when a warrior draws his sword and finishes his prey with a single stroke. Everything that does not add up is discarded instantly. Everything that adds up is maintained.

To be controlled is to be calm inside and to the fullest in your concentration and energy. It would seem that the Path of Self-control is a path of tranquility, and it is. Nonetheless, it is necessary to distinguish in a practical sense that being calm and peaceful inside does not mean being shutdown, warm or with low energy in your body. The body must be in its optimal state when your interior is in control of itself. To the fullest, with all its resources.

I remember once that a young man told me in a frustrated tone at the end of his tennis match, in which the scoreboard did not favor him:

> - "I could never control the moment during the match."

I just replied:

> - "In order to have control of your body you first need to have control of your soul, never the other way around."

I always ask a key question to the athletes who allow me to train them mentally and spiritually:

«Do you have control of winning?»

Most of them answer yes, and they explain to me that if they train properly, with discipline, eat well and commit to their sport, they will win. It seems that they are right, that if they do everything that is required to win they will win, however, that is completely false in reality. Nobody has control over winning, if that were true, everyone would win, and that would be impossible. Winning is not under our control, as there are factors -that are not under our control- that could prevent us from winning, such as the desire to win and ability of the other competitors or opponents.

There is no doubt that in life we should identify what is and what is not under our control. For instance, we cannot control the environment, nor the rest of the competitors' capacity, nor the judge's or arbitrator's decisions, nor people's beliefs or temperaments, not even some factors that could come up during our life, competitions or training.

On the other hand, we can control situations such as not surrendering to adversity or some injustice, making a perfect effort, being at peace with ourselves, controlling our emotions, living the moment with passion and intensity, remaining quiet and still when we should, etc. If one does what is under our control, without any truce, all the time, the odds of winning increase considerably. Yet, winning is not guaranteed. If we stop doing what is under our control, the odds of winning will undoubtedly decrease. The good news is that even if we do not win in a game or competition, if we do everything that is under our will or control, we will be winning for ourselves, but you must be aware of it.

Anyway, at the core of the philosophy that I practice and share, what I experience as an athlete, and what I teach to be lived in sports and life, is that what matters is not to win or lose. And I don't mean the typical phrase that says, *"The important thing is not to win but to compete."* This is not the philosophy or mentality practiced by a spiritual athlete. As I mentioned in the previous path, the important thing is not if you win, if you compete, or if you have a goal to achieve, the important thing is what you become as a person when you do it. There is the true essence of why one chooses a sport as an activity that adds up to one's life, as a person. What you become when you win or lose is what really counts, and that is achieved with emotional self-control and your inner peace while practicing your favorite sport. Our behavior and actions must be sown in the lives of other people.

To live in self-control consciousness is to live owning oneself. Each one of us decides how to feel, and self-control means not giving that power over your emotional state to someone else.

For instance, someone might insult me or compliment me, however, their comment is not what determines whether I feel offended or flattered, respectively. The one who determines or chooses how to feel with that kind of comment, is me. It is a choice and not a reaction.

Personally, I have always thought that a person out of control is like a drunken person. Drunk with their own emotion, so drunk that they don't know what they are saying, they are not being themselves.

Imagine that you are very frustrated and angry during a match, you "get so drunk" with your emotion, to the point of doing things that are taking you away from yourself. You insult yourself with your internal dialogue, you insult everything you think you are a victim of, you claim a possible offender, you cry out your anger, you offend, etc. As time passes, the state of drunkenness passes and you find yourself again sober from your emotions and controlled, remembering all those atrocities you did during your drunken state. Now what you have is a moral hangover of everything you did and everything you trampled over - starting with yourself- as a result of not controlling yourself.

This is the way emotions control you when you are not aware or when you do not realize that you are experiencing such emotion.

You need to prevent getting a blurry vision of your emotions and feelings. The difference between a blind person and an uncontrolled one, is that the blind person is aware that they don't see, while the other does not.

Emotional and spiritual intelligence is found while in control of emotions and mood. If you control your interior you can handle yourself with eloquence, intelligence, concentration and a lot of sense of the present.

Our control must be stronger than a hundred hurricanes together. Our character and calm must equal the storm.

A cold night with heavy rain, the Zen warrior was fighting in the middle of the battlefield. It was a fierce and bloody fight. There were hundreds of people around him and he hardly identified their faces in the dark. Shouts and whines were heard everywhere, he was unable to distinguish whether they came from partners or enemies. It smelled like wet earth, sweat and blood. There were women and children shouting and running to protect themselves, while the men fought against each other vigorously.

In the midst of all that chaos, the Zen warrior closed his eyes, took a deep breath and knelt down, feeling the mud on his legs. He raised his shield over his head and became aware of the moment. In that state of apparent absence, of calm and serenity, he stopped listening to everything that happened, focusing on his feelings and his being. There, serene, in peace and quiet, he could identify whether the hits on his shield came from a fighting partner or an enemy. So, just like that, with his eyes closed, he got up and used his lightsaber without doubting if he used it against an enemy or a partner. He could perfectly identify who they were. Always keeping calm inside, but with a lot of energy in his outer body.

I know athletes who want to concentrate on dominating the opponent before dominating themselves. They are so worried and busy wanting to win at any price, that they forget where the real strength is: having peace of mind and being resourceful. They are so immersed in being better as athletes, that they forget that they are damaging their integrity as persons. They believe that winning defines them as persons, which is absolutely false. What really defines you as a person are your actions during the game, your actions towards others, in real life and in the sports environment. Including your current opponent. Being out of control can lead you to do and/or say things that you would not do or say if you were under control.

If I was given the choice between being emotionally connected or physically connected, I would choose to be emotionally connected without hesitating. Something may go wrong with your body like a knee, a tendon, an arm, a shoulder, a muscle contracture, a cramp, etc.; but your head, mind, your peace and inner control should never, never, never fail you. In a lucid state, your mind will find unimaginable ways to overcome an adversity of your body and remain focused and connected with the moment.

Let's stop getting confused or get carried away by the environment, which is undoubtedly very seductive and attractive to the ego. What really determines who we are is our way of being. It will never be our successes, triumphs, positions in our jobs or popularity in school that define us. Self-control helps you not to trample over yourself while seeking a trophy, a medal or a prize.

The prize is a whim, you must surrender to that which controls you and that perhaps controls your entire life. Control of yourself is all you need.

Our heroic moments in life or in a competition are those in which we have the power to decide for solving what is needed when facing adversity. Resources are within ourselves. We don't need to govern anything in life, only ourselves. Let's be emotionally free with self-control.

HOW TO ACHIEVE THE PATH OF SELF-CONTROL

1. Be aware of your emotional state. This first step is very important.
2. If necessary, ask for help to identify your emotional state. Ask someone close to make you aware of your state. Avoid the mistake of telling the person who is helping you that what they are saying is not true. In those situations, be objective and identify the current state you are experiencing. The important thing is not having someone else identify your status, but that you are reminded that you should be aware of the state you experience at that time.
3. Find a neuronal anchor that reminds you that you must remain under control. It can be breathing and counting to ten

in a calm manner. Breathing is not necessarily for controlling yourself, but rather to remind you that you must be under control and aware of your state.

4. Stop defending other people's perspectives about your achievements, goals, or failures. Remain still and calm.

5. Never look for self-control outside. Stop collecting information from the outside and start collecting your own information from within. I mean your moods.

6. Once you have become familiar with identifying your emotional state, you can practice calm when chaos appears, pausing your emotions.

7. When you achieve self-control, start planning what you will do about it in the environment you're in. In that state of inner calm you can make intelligent decisions in a "sober" state.

CHAPTER 4

Path of Here and Now

«There is no beginning an no end, only present.»

- Ricardo Sala.

Because it is an exceptional state and to some extent inexplicable, defining the *"here and now"* is a challenge. Despite that, I venture to do it with the permission given to me by having experienced it many times.

Words do not exist in the *here and now,* yet, I will explain with words that sublime place and moment for the body, soul and spirit.

For me, *here and now* is a state of fulfillment without limits or restrictions. It is a state where the mind and its thoughts move away to allow everything to take a sense of present in which it is not necessary to add anything. It is a state where only the moment as such exists in all of its aspects. Your internal dialogue decreases its speed and number of words to let your body and senses flow and act in an unparalleled way. Literally, unparalleled. It is being 100% immersed in the experience you are living.

I wouldn't dare to say that the Path of *Here and Now* is my favorite, because it would be like putting the rest of the laws or paths on a lower plane. But I can say that it is a path which is reduced to absolute renunciation of thought. This state is precisely what is sought in spiritual training for an optimum and excellent development. When I train someone in the mental and spiritual fields, my goal will always be to teach them to enter the *here and now* and live it so that they notice the big difference between a "normal" action and a thoughtless action.

To be *here and now* means giving up the past, the future and time completely. It means giving up your own judgment, your own paradigms, limits and fears. There, in that place where only the moment exists, there are no beginnings or endings, there is no time, there are no results, there are no interpretations of the present, there are no questions or answers, you do not know your name, or who you are. Simply put, there is absolutely nothing to add. You literally become the moment. You stop being you to become the experience itself.

When an artist, an athlete or any person is performing an activity in which they are so focused and introduced in themselves, it means that they are in the *here and now.* For instance, when a painter is in front of his canvas and he is only flowing with the moment. He doesn't think anything, he just draws and paints in an exceptional way. He doesn't even think about it, he just does it. It is when a gymnast is performing his routine and does not think if he did any movement right or wrong, he does not think about his performance as such, he just performs it. It is when you are in front of your computer reading something that captivates you, and you are so into the reading that you don't know about anything else. These are moments when your mind is completely emptied of all those thoughts in order to act in an unimaginable way. Unlimited.

But, how did I arrive to be in and identify this sublime state of *here and now*? How did it happen? How did I manage to silence my mind to execute something almost unrecognizable with myself? It all started in my teens with a question that had no answer at that time. Every time I played sports, there was a person always present inside me, who spoke to me and sometimes even scolded me when I did something wrong; the same voice that congratulated me or cheered me when I did well, according to my self-evaluation of "good" and "bad".

One day I asked myself a question that changed my personal and sports life:

"Who am I really? The one who speaks or the one who listens to the scolding, congratulations or cheers? Who am I? Am I the one who asks the questions or the one who listens to them and who should answer?

We all have that internal dialogue that speaks to us and that comes from within. I knew that voice came from my mind, but I kept doubting who I really was. Some internal dialogues were very demanding, hard or negative, and others were more positive, depending on the context, but I still had the same question of who Ricardo really was, the one who was speaking or the one who was listening.

With that doubt I discovered that when I had my best moments of sports performance or any other school activity that was manual, the voice was silent and did not speak to me until the activity was over.

So, it was then that I decided to pay attention so I would notice when my inner voice was absent and when it came again. My entire learning process to silence my internal dialogue began with that doubt. The only thing I wanted was to silence it, since I discovered that I could do things better in silence. I could also see, hear and feel things that I didn't realize were there when my interior spoke to me. My inner voice distracted me from the action I was performing, although I thought I was concentrated. On the other hand, when my inner voice was gone, it was as if my own judge turned away from myself to let me be free and without limits. I was allowed to be in the *here and now.*

When I began to do it consciously, initially they were fleeting moments of states of *here and now*, where no one spoke and, in fact, I knew nothing about anything, I just practiced my sport and did it incredibly, effortlessly and fluently, I would literally turn into the action itself.

Afterwards I began to find people in the world who achieved these states of total disconnection with that inner voice, and I became much more excited about the subject. I discovered that it was not only a mental state, but that when such state was expressed more intensely and easily, it was because it was understood that it was a spiritual state.

To put it easily: it is a state where you don't think and yet you do what you do with greater capacity than you would if you were thinking.

Some sports psychologists call this "to be in the zone" or in states of high concentration. It is a good way to describe it, however, it is not quite like that or rather the description is incomplete. In said state of *here and now* you let go of your conscious mind, your ego, your thoughts, your own person, and that is no longer mental concentration, but an extremely spiritual state. So spiritual that the mind is not even present.

In the *here and now* you can achieve things that you would be surprised that you could do. In the *here and now* there are no explanations, you only do it, without knowing how, but you do it. Obviously, you do things that you already know how to do, but with improved execution and with sensations that you would not notice if your mind was present speaking to you. When you are there, in the strict present, you are alert and effortless. It is the only moment alive. When it is about being in the *here and now*, neither the past nor the future are invited to that place and moment.

TAKE OUT THE TRASH

I perfectly share the comment of the spiritual master Dan Millman (former American Olympic gymnast) when he said that you have to take out the garbage from the mind to get the body to do things at an unimaginable level. That is, take out the garbage to achieve states of *here and now*. Talking to Dan at an event where we were both speakers, we talked about the necessity of emptying the mind of all the pollution that prevents you from really feeling the experience in order to achieve the state of *here and now.*

Something extraordinary is happening at all times, but you don't realize it because of all the pollution you have in your mind that doesn't allow you to enjoy the present. For this reason, it is common for me to insist on telling people and athletes who I coach spiritually to constantly *"take out the trash,"* and they perfectly know that I mean the trash in their head. It's another way of saying: clean and clear your mind.

Trash is identified as any type of thought that has to do with the past, future, with the way in which you are going to execute an action, with the result of the action, with the judgment you make of the result of your action or with any other thought of process or ego.

But, what does emptying your mind mean? What does taking out the trash mean? Taking out the trash, or emptying your mind, is to stop thinking about the past or the future, and without any effort, focusing on everything that happens in the current moment, experiencing a state of isolation and peace connected 100% with what exists at that precise moment.

Something is always happening, at all times and in all places. Never, never, never do impressive events stop happening. With a clear mind, you stop thinking of who you are, you stop thinking about your past mistakes and about your mental projections of the future. For athletes it means to stop thinking about the scoreboard while you execute or on any parameter while you are performing the activity. It is to stop thinking about the result, since the result lies in the future and not in the present. Trash is all those thoughts that draw you away from the only thing that matters, from this moment, from *here and now.*

When your status passes *here and now* while performing an action, and you realize that you are no longer there, you are immediately filled again with dozens of thoughts and unfortunately you miss out on everything that is happening at that moment.

WHAT IS THE MOST IMPORTANT TIME, POINT OR PLAY IN SPORTS?

It is also very common for the people I train to ask:

What is the most important point? What is the most important play? What is the most important competition of your season? What is the most important training of your preparation? What is the most important shot in a game?

And the answer on my part is always and always will be the same: the one you carry out.

I remember once training a girl with a prominent professional future in golf, I asked her:

> - "What is the most important shot in golf?"

> - "Well there are several, a very important one is when exiting the hole, the driver. But also when you are on the green, a shot there counts a lot" -she replied.

> To which I commented:

> -"Your biggest lesson today in your mental and spiritual training will be the

following: it doesn't matter if you are at the exit of each hole, on the green or anywhere in the field, your most important shot will always be the one that you are going to execute in that precise moment, in the *here and now*. There should be no other shot in your mind other than the one you are going to execute." -

In tennis, I would tell you the same thing, that the next point will always be the most important one and the only one in the whole game. The same in golf and in any sport of points or shots. And the next play will always be the most important one in sports such as soccer or football. In baseball, the next pitch will be the most important one of the entire game. And so on, in all sports. In sports such as running, cycling or triathlon this would mean that the most important step, pedaling, stroke or yard is the one you are doing at that moment, not at the beginning, not at the end, but the one you are executing.

It's easy to understand: leave the last shot or the previous move behind and focus on the next move. Anyone can understand that easily, right? However, not everyone achieves that because of the excessive habit of thinking. A kind of addiction to having internal dialogue.

Practice the vital principle: *"The next point or moment is the most important of all";* it is giving up everything. To give up emotions from the previous point means to give up the scoreboard, to give up the judgment that your own self made of the past execution, to give up some mistake from the judge or referee, to give up fatigue, to give up your internal dialogue, your ego, it is to renounce your own being, so that once empty of all that garbage and being clean inside you, you face the next point or moment. You decide that state of excellence, it is under your control, but it requires a lot of practice.

There are self-sabotages in your conscious mind, since it wants with all its strength to be there, to be the protagonist and prevent you from achieving the desired *here and now.*

Consciousness wishes to get credit and recognition of what you are doing, when in fact itself could be in some way hindering the execution process. The way in which your conscious mind supports your execution is by staying away and taking the role of a simple spectator. Like a parent or coach: since you already know how to do something, you can do it freely without it giving additional instructions at the moment. It can give them to you, just like the conscious mind, but never when you are carrying out the action.

But why, if it is so easy to understand, not everyone can do it? Because outside there are so many things and information with emotions that they don't allow you to reach within yourself. The good news is that it is possible and that state of *here and now* can be achieved, you just have to do it and practice to master it, like everything in life. Constant practice and training are what is needed to make this state easier and longer-lasting every time. That is why it is important to constantly take out the garbage and clean your mind before any execution, however short it may be, like a golf shot, or however long it may be, like in an ultra marathon or an Ironman triathlon.

In that state of *here and now,* wherever you are, just relax mentally and the pressure will vanish, your ego will melt and that's when your mask falls down and your true self appears. And why is it necessary to relax? Because there is nothing to worry about, there is no tension because no goal or result will define you or should be in that present. There is nothing beyond, you just have to live and "be" the moment.

A spiritual warrior meditates in every action by freeing himself from all bonds and of the addiction to think and speak at all times. He renounces the belief of knowing everything, he even renounces the belief that he is an expert in something that he is said to be an expert in. The first step is to be in the "not-knowing anything" mode, because a spiritual warrior is not an expert in anything, he is free of labels, much less does he believe he is perfect or seeks such perfection or victory. A warrior is pure vulnerability and that is his greatest value. Lowering your guard is the first step to silence your mind.

I constantly tell people to look for excellence, but not perfection. A warrior is not perfect nor seeks perfection, since no one has ever been perfect and no one will ever be. So, what makes them think they should be? Believing that they must be perfect is a very common mistake in society and in athletes. In the *here and now* everything is renounced, including perfection. Excellence and continuous improvement of a skill are sought, whether in the body or mind, but especially in the spirit. However, the concept of spiritual excellence is different. Spiritual excellence is giving up everything in order to enjoy the abundance of the present and your interior. In the excellence of the *here and now* there are only actions of the strict present.

In the *here and now* you never know what will happen nor will you find the end of the action because there are simply no endings. The present moment is the entire trip as such, and precisely it is in that place and in that space where happiness lies. If you discover that happiness lies in the final destination it means that you are not in the present. If you feel serenity in the present with what you are doing and with what is happening, without thinking about it, just feeling peace, joy, calmness in your actions, in your executions and feeling fluent, you are experiencing happiness.

In the *here and now* each movement is made for the movement's sake, each action for the action, not for the result or score you give it. Nor will it ever be done for what others think of you or your execution, it should only be done for the real pleasure of doing so. Either way, win or lose, you will remain exceptional and greater than any moment or competition.

HOW TO ACHIEVE THE PATH OF HERE AND NOW

1. To silence the internal dialogue with your mind, start with short periods of

meditation. If at the beginning you cannot silence your mind or you struggle, lean on some guided meditation or someone who teaches you to meditate. You can find guided meditations on Spotify, YouTube or on some other meditation platforms.

2. Increase the duration of your meditation sessions, however, initially it is more important to have short but constant periods - at least once a day-, that long periods only once a week. Practice must be constant and daily.

3. Practice yoga. Yoga is very useful since you are executing physical postures, but meditating with your mind clean. No trash. That will help you to be on the move, but quiet, just as it happens in sports.

4. When you get in your car -without it moving- pay 100% attention to your experience. Sharpen your senses. You will stop thinking by focusing on everything you do and what surrounds you. Your relaxed mind must be

present in every movement, in every feeling, in every sound. Pay attention to what your hands feel on the steering wheel, your feet on the pedals, the smell of the interior, etc. Remain in that state for a few minutes. When you master it, move on to the next level. Now drive your car paying attention and focusing 100% on everything that is happening. Put your view in panoramic mode, pay attention to all the internal and external sounds of the car, feel your feet, hands, breath and everything that is kinesthetic. Do so until the words in your head disappear and you can drive while maintaining that state. Your peripheral vision of the outside will help you to be in the *here and now.*

5. Do the same as in step four, but executing your sports activity. Sharpen all your senses and focus on some element of your environment without judgments or attachments, for instance in the sport of tennis, on the ball. If it's

golf, you can also focus on the ball, but in both cases avoid thinking in the execution of your shot. Just do it with infinite confidence, quiet and without garbage. Add the application of the Law of Fluency right there to carry out your movement. In sports like running, swimming or cycling, pay attention to everything around you, without thinking, just living it.

6. Scan your body constantly. If you identify any judgment after your execution it means that you are not in the *here and now.* Remember that any word you say that has to do with the past or future is pollution. Clean your mind constantly with the same practice and result you obtained in meditation.

7. Keep the peace and serenity at all times when you are in the *here and now,* applying the Path of Self-control at the same time.

8. While running, cycling or swimming, relax by breathing. Loosen your muscles without decreasing the

intensity, and in that moment of relaxation, sharpen all your senses. If a thought comes, immediately stop listening to it by raising the volume to the sounds you hear.

9. The next time you go are going to eat your food, just focus and send your awareness to the taste of your first bite. Pay attention to the size of the bite you gave, to the temperature and texture of the food, to the different flavors it may have. Chew it with ease and enjoy it as if it were the last bite of your life. Keep that state effortlessly, very calm and peaceful. Continue like this until you manage to finish your meal doing the same with each bite. If there are no words coming from you while you eat, you will have been in the *here and now.*

10. Watch a sunrise or sunset without judging it. Just look at it in all its color. Observe it first in peripheral view, the entire picture. Get lost in its beauty and put aside any thoughts that have to do

with details of the landscape. Later, without words inside you, just start observing the details. Remember to do it without haste, without hurries and without the sense of time. Just surrender to its beauty, breathing slowly and deeply. You can repeat point number 10 with any landscape, be it the sea, a river, the mountains, the moon or anything beautiful that our universe shows us.

Remember that something is always happening, always, always, *here and now.*

CHAPTER 5

Path of Potentiality or Karma

«No one escapes the effects of their actions.»

- Ricardo Sala.

The Law of Potentiality or Karma is also called the Law of Cause and Effect. How we act, we receive.

As a scientist, at first it seemed complex or subjective to prove the Law of Karma. Nonetheless, I managed to prove it, otherwise the present path would not be in this book. Numerous spiritual materials speak of things like: *"If you act well, you will do well"* and *"If you act ill, there will be misfortunes in your life."*

Oriental philosophies mention that if you act well and the effect of goodness is not fulfilled, it is because you are paying for another life, or that you will receive that good in a future life. As I mentioned earlier, for a scientist like me, that is difficult or impossible to verify. I have no way of remembering a past life and I will not remember anything in my future life, for that reason, I will not speak of Karma in reincarnations. I will talk about the spiritual Karma that I have been able to verify through results throughout the last years of my life. In other words: I will talk about a real karma, verifiable, proven and which I live daily.

I have precisely changed the word "Karma" to the word *"potentiality"*, so that said Karma is clearer to live and explain.

As stated by its definition, Karma is the Law of Cause and Effect. The *cause* is the action itself and the *effect* is the experience. On some occasions it is met immediately and on other occasions it is met at a different time, but it doesn't matter, it is always fulfilled. The first case is like cashing a check at the bank immediately; and the other case is as if you're going to collect a promissory note, but without a specific payment date. The payment you will receive will be dependant on the action you have taken, whether of goodness, indifference or evil.

Like all spiritual laws in this book, the present one applies not only to sports but to life itself. Karma is everywhere and at all times, believe it or not.

Summarized in a common phrase, let's say that karma is: *"What you sow, you reap."* However, there's nothing spiritual in it, it is a law of life that happens every moment, whether you agree or not.

But where is the spiritual part in Karma? It lies in removing from your mind the belief that everything is a sort of business in which I act well because I know that I will do well, without it coming from the heart, but from the calculating brain that does it for its own good. Stop thinking about the instant or future benefit you will have, and feel the outcome of the same moment, as a satisfying experience that you and others have. For this reason, I wanted to use the word *potentiality* to explain how the phenomenon of Karma happens.

The Path of Potentiality or Karma means that depending on how you decide to treat people or nature, you will receive the same feeling and experience in return.

Example:

If I arrive at a cafe to ask for a drink, and I kindly ask for it by starting with a heartfelt greeting, asking questions like: "How have you been?", accompanied by a smile and good energy, I will receive in return the same: good treatment, good energy and good attitude from the clerk. At that time the Law of Karma and Potentiality was fulfilled. It was immediate. I didn't need that kindness with which I approached the clerk to be met in the future. And above all, I felt very good doing it and receiving back good energy.

But what happens if the clerk, despite my good energy and vibes, does not respond the same and addresses me in a bad mood because he was already like this? Well, it happens that Karma was fulfilled anyway, even if it doesn't seem so, since I felt all my goodness in deciding to address him with a good attitude. Remember, it is not a contract in which I act to receive, it is my own decision to want to be in a state of goodness to achieve a state of goodness in my own experience, not necessarily in another person. Goodness is delivered and at that moment you feel goodness. If you insist on treating him well, even if the person is moody, the chances of a change in his attitude are greatly increased, since the field of potentialization is in action. Who is harder to love is who needs it the most. Let us give love to whom it seems the most difficult to do so.

If you have a problem with someone in life, treat them better than anyone so that the Law of Potentialization acts and the person has a greater chance of acting in the sense that you vibrate. On the other hand, if you have a problem with someone and you decide not to treat them well because they "don't deserve it," guess which Law of Potentialization was activated? Yes, that of the other person, since Karma works for both ends. Your unwanted attitude or grumpy energy will be the one that takes possession of the experience itself and of yourself. It is like a magnetic field.

After such explanation, we can now talk about Karma or the Path of Potentialization focused on sports. Where and when does Karma appear? The answer is at all times and everywhere.

Karma is a current and permanent state that has to do with decisions. It is the ability to feel the outcome of your actions and the effect it will have on your spiritual and energetic state. We are making decisions all the time. We have 70,000 thoughts a day on average, and in each of them there is Karma. Karma appears when you are about to make the decision to choose a cerrtain path and have the ability to see the end of it before traveling it. It is instantaneous and it is still in the *here and now*. If you don't like the feeling at the end of that path, don't make that decision and don't do it. If you like the outcome, do it. So simple and easy. It is a feeling in the heart and not in the mind.

Do you want a person to treat you well? Treat them well. Do you want someone to respect you? Respect them. Do you want someone to smile at you? Smile at them. Do you want your opponent to have a good attitude towards you? Have a good attitude with them. Do you want someone to be glad when they see you? See them gladly. Do you want your children to be polite? Be polite with them. Do you want a better world? Be good to the world. Want love? Give love.

You cannot expect someone to respect you if you don't respect them, unless that someone is more spiritual than you and respects you, even if you don't. And you know what? The chances that you will end up respecting them will increase, because the Law of Potentiality works like that.

You cannot expect love from someone you do not love or mistreat. It is as if you had orange trees in your garden and expect them to give apples. It would be absurd and unnatural.

THE IMPORTANCE OF THE HEART

The heart plays an important role in the Law of Karma. It is vital. Much more than the mind. The mind follows the heart's order. The heart is a highly sensory, intuitive, holistic organ. The heart does not have a win-or-lose orientation. If you feel that way, it is not the heart that speaks, but the mind. The heart constantly exchanges energy. When you compete, exchange good energy from the heart so that you see and feel the potential that your body will have. Compete with negative thoughts and you will receive unwanted energy. Compete with the mental feeling of wanting to beat someone else no matter what, and you will see how difficult it will be. Even your energy will not be the best to achieve it, because it is not focused on potentializing an optimal experience, therefore, the Law of Potentialization will act against you, but only because of your decision.

Compete with kindness, feeling that if someone else wins, you will feel something good. You will realize how different it feels.

Once, in a spiritual coaching I was doing with a 16-year-old boy who plays tennis, frustrated after a game he lost, he told me:

> - "This can't be! Each ball that hit the other's line was marked as out! So, I started to get desperate, angry, frustrated and I lost the game."

He knows perfectly what the Law of Karma or Potentiality means, since I am his coach, so I just told him:

> - "Remember, you are responsible for your despair, anger and frustration, nobody else is. You lacked the ability to see the outcome of the decision you made when you entered that mood."

> - "I didn't decide anything, I just felt it."

- "Karma is being aware and awake, otherwise, you will simply be at the mercy of your emotion. You must act, not react." -I answered.

-- "And if I hadn't been angry, would my opponent have stopped cheating?"

- "I don't know" -I replied-, "however, you do not need to control your opponent or control his mind. You should not control anything or anybody because it will not be possible. You cannot control a tree and decide when it blooms and what kind of fruits it gives. It is nature and we are nature. The only one you need to control is yourself. Control your mind, with the help of your heart."- I concluded.

What the boy needed was to create, by choice, the desired energy field. This can also be supported and helped by the Path of Self-control. The Law of Potentialization is fulfilled sooner or later, much sooner than later.

When you do something, when you are about to make a decision, take the heart into account, a lot. It will give you many clues and advice. Hence the word "hunch." But, does the heart never go wrong? Yes, it does go wrong, but it is the organ that makes the least mistakes of your whole body. I suggest you go to it frequently.

Once, the Zen warrior was riding slowly in the forest. He was accompanied by other partners from the village and at that moment he met a former battle brother who had betrayed him. He hadn't seen him since his betrayal. The Zen warrior approached him, got off his horse, and with a smile on his face and a lot of energy, he greeted him fraternally, along with a hug. His former friend was surprised at such a compassionate greeting and reciprocated in the same way. After chatting for a moment, the warrior wished him well and said goodbye, and he let him know that the next time he passed through the village he would invite him over to his house for dinner. The old friend thanked him for the gesture, smiled and nodded. They said goodbye and each one followed his path.

After a few minutes, one of the Zen warrior's partners who accompanied him asked:

> - "Wasn't that guy the one who betrayed you?"
> - "Yes, he is." -said the warrior.
> - "But, why do you treat him like this?" - he said amazed.
> - "Was there any other way to do it?"- replied the warrior, ending the conversation.

Karma is giving what you would like to have in return, but from the bottom of your heart. If you don't do it that way, you will still receive Karma, but not the best one for your own self.

I want to make it clear and warn that the heart is extremely useful in this path. In matters of falling in love and attachments you will also have to rely on your mind so they can work as a team. They both work very well together, only that each one is an expert in their own field. Just like the heart is in the Law of Potentialization or Karma.

If you want success in your life and in sports, be aware of your decisions. Flow with kindness and you will feel kindness.

Practice the Path of Karma or Potentiality and over time your accounts receivable will be more than your accounts payable.

HOW TO ACHIEVE THE PATH OF KARMA OR POTENTIALITY

1. Be aware of your decisions. Let them be choices and not reactions. When you make a decision stop a little to analyze it. Start by practicing and carrying out the habit of greeting every person that crosses your way, every day. Smile and greet them. If you make this a habit, you will gradually begin to feel the Law of Karma.
2. Treat someone with whom you have a kind of problem with a lot of love and

positive details. Give love to whom it seems the most difficult to do so.

3. When you are in a competition event, try to cross a rival's path. Say hello and wish them good luck from the bottom of your heart, along with a hug or sincere handshake.

4. When the competition is over, greet your opponents and congratulate them, especially if they succeeded. Do it with all the sincerity of your own being.

5. Before making a decision, have the ability to see the future, the different types of outcomes you might have. This is done by your mind, however, go straight to your heart and analyze the state you will have in the outcomes. If you feel well-being or joy, do it and make that decision, otherwise, if you don't feel it, then don't do it.

6. Surprise the people that surround you with something that has to do with kindness. It can be helping them, hugging them or anything that has to do

with them feeling that they count on you
at all times.

Remember that this training of the Path of
Potentiality or Karma is for your own self. Do
not expect thanks or good attitude from the
people with whom you are going to practice it.
Do not expect anything in exchange for your
karmatic state. The experience must be
exclusively your own, personal.

CHAPTER 6

Path of Fluency

«Never try, just do it.»

- Ricardo Sala.

The Path of Fluency is aimed at saving energy, or allocating it to the right place for greater bodily and mental efficiency. It means that everything must be done with the least possible physical and mental effort. Any sign of effort at the exterior (bodily) or inner (mental) level means that there is something creating resistance in your performance and it will not be optimal.

Moments are as they are. I especially mean the adverse ones. If you oppose or resist to what is happening it can cause you discomfort, extra tiredness or even suffering. Accepting the moment with everything there is is the key. Accept everything there is, relax and stop fighting against the flow or else, you will waste energy in a fight that will wear you out uselessly. Accept what is coming to your body, to your life and stop resisting so you can achieve a better performance with fluency and peace.

Every time I teach the Law of Fluency to an athlete, they just can't hide the look in their faces when I tell them that all activity is done effortlessly. They immediately ask me this kind of questions:

"How am I going to run up a mountain effortlessly?" - "How do I pedal up a steep hill without effort?" - "How do I make a final sprint effortlessly?"

They think it is illogical, yet it is not so when you understand and practice the Law of Fluency.

The Path of Fluency means that there shouldn't be anything that causes resistance inside. It is to flow in body and mind. It is to relax and stop worrying, but still giving your best with your body. You feel that your muscles, bones and joints are working naturally, in harmony and effortlessly. It is feeling complete peace and fluidity in your body, spirit and mind.

Let's think about our mother nature for a moment and observe her behavior. The grass does not try to grow or struggles to grow, it only grows despite any adversity; the birds don't try to fly, they just fly effortlessly; the Earth spins effortlessly at millions of miles per hour; fish swim effortlessly; the tree blooms in spring and undresses in autumn effortlessly. Nature does not try to do anything, it just does it, despite any situation, favorable or unfavorable.

Under that principle or natural rule, human beings should be the same. Putting aside the thoughts of "trying" is a first step. One "tries" when learning a new activity with which the mind and body are not familiar. It is a temporary process, not a permanent one. Once the body and mind become familiar with the new ability, they stop trying and simply do it.

Think about the activity of walking. Walking is an activity that had its process once. When we were babies we found it hard to learn it, but we did. Just like a bird that comes out of its shell or a newborn deer that wants to walk, it took us a while to learn to walk. In the beginning we "try" to walk, but now we don't try, we just do it effortlessly and naturally. It is exactly the same with all the activities and skills that we already perform naturally. Running, swimming, cycling or any other activity must be done naturally, be it up, down, at maximum speed, or against air or current. The ability to do so is intact, natural.

The issue is brought up when you think you need effort to face something that has a higher level of difficulty. Something that requires greater strength, endurance and in which sometimes our body gives us signs of muscle pain. For some it may seem that even suffering comes when making maximum efforts above their capacity.

What does nature do when facing adversity? What does a palm tree do on the beach when a hurricane comes? What does a tree that faces a fierce wind do? Both the tree and the palm tree just let go. They bend without resisting. They would never fight against the wind, as they would create resistance and break. The tree and the palm tree accept the moment and show no defense against the wind. They don't try to face the moment, they just do it, naturally, until the moment passes. So you must act in the face of adversity in your physical activity. You must flow with the moment, regardless of whether there are adversities or a sort of need to try harder.

How does the Path of Fluency work? Why do we have surprising results and our body has a better performance when we practice it? Simple: our energy is not directed or spent on issues that are not necessary. There is no mistaken redirection of energy to an issue or part of your body or thoughts that are not necessary.

Imagine that your body has a 100,000-watt battery. It will be the equivalent of our vital energy. When we are training or in a competition, we need our body's battery to be able to carry out the activity. It is an activity that is not part of your regular daily activities, therefore it will require extra battery. Suppose we are running on a flat surface with no inclination at an aerobic pace. A bit after, we have to run uphill and it becomes an anaerobic activity. The air starts to run out and the muscles start to burn, especially in the legs. If you go up without using the Law of Fluency, signs of resistance will begin to appear inside you. First, you will have difficulty breathing naturally. Then there will be signs of resistance such as hard legs and even your body language changes. Gestures of effort on your face and maybe thoughts of some kind of struggle within you. Let's say you are not having a good time at that moment and you are still "trying" to move forward however you can hoping for the moment to pass. All the signs of resistance that I mentioned require energy to manifest, in other words, you spend vital energy for them to exist. You could be using that energy somewhere else where it would be useful, yet it goes elsewhere because nothing is flowing, not within you - mind and spirit,- neither outside -body-. In this state of resistance there is discomfort in achieving the objective. There is definitely no harmony at that time.

With resistance you get tired faster. With resistance your energy watts are uselessly used in places that are not necessary. That is the reason for premature fatigue. If you train like this and you think it is normal to have that kind of effort, wait until you experience the Path of Fluency so that you feel and see how tiredness does come, but in a different way and much later.

The Path of Fluency has the benefit of saving energy. This path teaches you to create, store and use your energy efficiently, without unnecessary leaks.

The same happens in your daily life. When you look for power or control over people, you spend energy. When you seek to sustain your importance as a person, you spend energy, and a lot of it. When the ego requires its nourishment to be the approval you need from the rest of the people, you spend energy. When we seek a goal for personal gain only, you also spend energy.

Reality is you are acting against nature and you will never defeat it. You are going against a natural flow. You and I are nature, we are part of a common whole that requires connection, not exclusion or fight against it, like the tree facing the wind.

Clean your mind constantly, empty it. When you are competing, become immune to criticism. Stop being afraid of the challenge you face and flow with it. The challenge is part of yourself, it is within you, flow with it, just feel and execute your activity effortlessly. Think that everything is natural. Relax your mind and body, literally feel that there is no effort. Start from relaxed breathing, even if you feel you are short of breath. Breathe and think that it is an activity that your body is familiar with. Connect your mind and thoughts with your muscles so they work in harmony. Each cell should be at peace and quiet, all performing together the activity that apparently seems to wear you out. Relax your muscles while giving your maximum capacity in your body. Stop gesturing with your face, relax all of its muscles and flow. It seems contradictory, but your body must be giving everything it has and at the same time inside you there is no sense of effort.

Your vital energy multiplies when you perform your actions in harmony and self-esteem; in harmony and love with other human beings; in harmony and love with nature; in harmony and love with the universe and God; they become an unlimited source of energy. It is as if you had an internal battery of 100,000 million watts and you are charging it automatically and constantly.

CONNECT WITH YOUR NATURAL ENVIRONMENT

The Path of Fluency always works best when you are connected to your natural environment. Never feel resistance against anything around you. Not against things, nor people, situations, places. Stop evaluating or rating the environment as good, bad, ideal, etc. Instead of evaluating, connect with the energy of the moment and live it. If you swim, connect with the water and enter its flow, do not fight against it. If you run or cycle with wind against or in favor, enter the molecules of the same wind and camouflage with them. If you are in a storm of rain or sand in the desert, do not fight against it, become it and flow. Even if it seems that you are going against its energy, reality is that resistance is what leads you not to flow. For this reason, relax and keep executing your activity as when the tropical palm tree relaxes when facing the hurricane.

Personally, what leads me to practice the Path of Fluency is thinking that my body is gaseous rather than solid when I run, but without losing its shape. That makes me a lighter being. In addition, I think of Ricardo as a child, when I was 9 or 10 years old, and weighed 20 kilos. Innocent. The one who didn't think if it was uphill or downhill, the one who didn't judge his natural environment, the one who loved to feel the wind or the rain on his face without thinking about anything but fun. That is me today when I play sports, and it is the kind of mental state that I recommend to people who I train on the spiritual field.

Being a 6 to 8-year-old child has many advantages. For example, at that age you do not compete fiercely as a teenager or adult would. Personally, being a child makes me free by just performing the activity without thinking if the result defines me as a person. Actually, I don't think about the result at all, just like when I went out to play or ride a bike on the street of my childhood. At that age there are no worries. The biggest worry was wishing that it wouldn't get dark so that I wouldn't have to go back home and stop playing. As a child there is a smile on the face, far from excessive effort. Children do everything and believe that they can do everything because they are not yet told -or do not know- they can't do it. Simply put, a child's attitude goes more towards the sense of flow than that of resistance.

Practice the Path of Fluency so that your energy and performance increase. May that as it be, the greatest benefit is found during the process of carrying out the activity, where there is only ease and spiritual calmness. Same in life.

HOW TO ACHIEVE THE PATH OF FLUENCY

1. Start with your mind. Relax it and release it from any thoughts of resistance. Breathe easily. Focus and direct your awareness towards your breath. Breathe naturally, effortlessly and as deeply as you can. It doesn't

matter what activity or effort you feel you are doing.

2. While performing the activity that costs you effort, relax those muscles that you feel that are working and where you feel resistance, but without decreasing the intensity of the activity. Let's say that on the outside you are giving your maximum capacity and at the same time, inside you, you are going at peace and relaxation.

3. Connect with nature. Feel that you are going inside everything that surrounds you, that you are part of a whole. Feel that you flow with everyone and everything.

4. When you perform your sports activity, feel light, regardless of the weight of your body or things that you carry. Make your mind do the work and think that you are a light child performing an effortless activity, without attachments, just flowing.

5. Scan your body constantly during the activity and locate places where you

need more energy or that require eliminating internal struggles. For example, if you are performing an activity in which you are very short of breath and have a hard time breathing, focus your awareness on the chest, and just focus on that place thinking that you need to unblock anything that does not allow you to breathe. The mind is very powerful. Just think that you are sending energy to that place and that your cells are energized by focusing your mind to that place. Think that the inner struggle fades and that it becomes natural. I personally use colors. When I start to feel tired in a specific place in my body, I imagine that my cells and molecules are red and that they need help. Once I have located the places that need harmony by scanning them mentally, I send signals with my thoughts, relaxing, so that they are cleaned and changed to blue. I just think about it and let my mind do its job. Blue cells and molecules are the optimal ones and the red ones are the ones that require "cleaning."

6. Start with daily ten-minute sessions of meditation so that you begin to enjoy moments of stillness and inner silence where there is nothing, no attachments, nor thoughts, nor words, just flow and connection with the moment.
7. Keep increasing the time of the meditation sessions.

Peaceful Miles   Ricardo Sala

CHAPTER 7

Path of Humbleness

«Everything that is alive is on the same level.»

- Ricardo Sala.

I define humbleness as the mental and spiritual state of being on the same level as people and as living beings. I am on the same level as you, as everyone and as everything that is alive. No one or nothing is above or below anyone. No one is more, nor is anyone less.

Humbleness is based on the fact that no one has a higher rank as a person, regardless of achievements, knowledge, possessions, skills, appearances or social status. If someone comes to believe that they are superior, it is because their pride tempted them to cover some lack of psychological and spiritual self-esteem of their being.

One who feels inferior to someone also lacks humbleness by simply placing themselves on a level of inequality, different from others.

In both cases, feeling superior or inferior is due to personal insecurities and lack of self-worth by cause of the ego and its unique identification with its "I."

To be humble is to win or lose a game and not feel superior or inferior to anything or anyone. To be humble is to lose a game and acknowledge from the bottom of our heart what has been accomplished and congratulate our opponent for their victory. To be humble is to win and make the opponent feel that it was a matter of the game and not a matter of themselves as persons. To be humble is to minimize your achievements in the comparison level with other beings, preventing the ego from diminishing your being.

I remember once when things were turning out to win a competition and somebody from the press came and told me:

> - "You are the best and there is no one who has been able to approach your level. What can you tell us about it?"
> - "Thank you! I feel very good; however, it was only today that I arrived first. And only in this competition." I replied.

You should never misunderstand that if you win you are the best for an extended period of time. You have to be aware that you were only the best among those who competed, that particular day and in that competition. Besides, you only came first today, we don't know about tomorrow.

Obviously, you enjoy the moment, celebrate, and reap the fruits of your work. That is a pleasure that is enjoyed and one feels fulfilled in one's goals. Anyhow, I think of it as if there were several boxes inside my mind and only in one of those boxes did I win or lose. It does not have any influence on the rest of the labeled boxes of values, of the self, of what a person is. If I win in one of those boxes or compartments, it does not affect the others. That is, if I win a mountain race, it does not mean that I also won in triathlon or cycling, or that it makes me a better son or a better brother or a better person. Each one of these boxes correspond to an activity that I perform and all of them are in a larger box called SPIRITUAL BEING. We are spiritual beings with human experiences, and not human beings with spiritual experiences.

The reflection made is that humbleness places you on the following: you only won that day, in that competition and in that sport. And most important of all: you are the same as everyone else, only with a preparation and a skill that led you to reach the final goal first that day. That's all, there is no more.

A humble person is simple in spirit. They are austere when they talk about themselves. If they communicate something about their achievements, abilities or knowledge, they do so with the only kind intention of giving and sharing to add value to the person who genuinely cares about their actions or life.

We have to be humble in order to be kind from the bottom of our hearts. Whomever is humble is kind, because there are no distinctions or levels, it is as if they were speaking to themselves when they are speaking to others. We must give and share everything we have within, without ego and without expecting anything in return. Being humble gives you a way of life in which value adds to you, and the saying that "anyone can", that if you do something that someone else still can't, that doesn't mean you are unique. When being humble, feeling unique is not part of your lifestyle.

You must be aware that happiness is not found in a trophy, but in a decision of your own coming from your heart. You don't find happiness in the shape of things or people, rather the opposite, you find it in everything that has no physical form.

When you practice humbleness, and let's say that you are a person who does extraordinary things, someone else may come to believe that you are superior because of your abilities and achievements. Nonetheless, a humble person is always with their feet on the ground, without ego and in their security status. Because humbleness makes you sure of who you are. Only you can achieve such security through humbleness. When someone praises you, use humor and healthy sarcasm to minimize your achievements which other people comment, so you will mentally place those people on a level of equality between you and them.

Never settle praise in your mind or heart. Smile at it and let it pass like a tourist who is passing through a country, accepting and thanking for their visit, but without inviting it to stay to live there. Praise should be as fleeting as possible so that it cannot lift you from the ground level. Always think and act in the scope of equal positions.

The humble person, when practicing the equality of being, feels no shame in helping everyone who crosses their path. There are no secrets for anyone. They share the formulas of their success without any objection because they are convinced of spiritual abundance and not lack of opportunities. Humbleness does not mean to have little, on the contrary, humbleness is to be rich in your actions, thoughts and soul.

If you want your life, sports or non-sports, to walk the Path of Abundance of spirituality, you must practice humbleness by renouncing the false belief of inequality and that you are a special being compared to other living beings, or that you find yourself above or below others. Humbleness is an attitude of impartiality.

Master, educate and tame your ego. No being practices humbleness better than one who has been taming and transcending the ego to remain in the purest state of their being.

Being humble is not comparing yourself to someone else and resulting favorable or unfavorable against others. It may be that someone else is better or worse than you in some skill, development or knowledge, but they will never be better or worse than you as a person. We are all the same. When comparing yourself as a person, your own lack of security comes out. If you are not humble, you will believe that you are one of the few who can do something extraordinary, believing yourself to be special or unique.

The humble person teaches others to achieve what they can or could do at some time. They share knowledge on the same personal level. The humble person believes in the relevance that everyone who desires something that they have already achieved is possible for everyone as well.

The humble person is much more understanding, tolerant, kind, cooperative, generous, friendly, and above all , shares more than the person entrenched in their ego, in their assumptions and their desire for people to know what they are doing, believing mistakenly that they are what they do, and in the constant energetic defense of their selfish structure.

Humbleness teaches you to identify and meet the needs of others. A humble being shines on their own, without the need to talk, or the temptation to shout to be noticed.

By practicing humbleness you become a balanced being and it places you in the real qualities you have. A humble person does not need makeup for the soul, and if they run into an arrogant person, they feel blissful in their humbleness and do not present a single mental sign of wanting to talk about themselves. Humbleness offers you that.

You must be humble in order to find out that happiness does not depend on what you or others can do or have. One who is humble does not practice envy, on the contrary, the achievements of others are also their achievements, feeling just as happy as whoever achieved it. For the humble, the happiness of others is also their happiness, since we are connected in a state of equality.

On another occasion, a radio announcer asked me:

- "Who is more complete, an ironman athlete or an ultra-distance runner?"
- "The most complete is the who believes that one is not better than the other." - I replied.

The Zen warrior does not have shortcomings or insecurities. His own humbleness leads him to sit at night, around the bonfire, to share his victories with humbleness and give everything necessary to motivate the rest of his peers so that they can also achieve it, and that he himself is no more nor better than them. The warrior is an open book to be read by anyone, since he writes his experiences, battles, triumphs and defeats for all , knowing perfectly that what he does does not make him special. What makes him enlightened is his humbleness, the intangible, that which has no physical form.

The Zen warrior does not live or fight to be better than others. He fights against his enemy, the ego, to defeat it; and in each victory or defeat he learns, shares his learning and his experience. He lives for the pleasure of living and then he shares it without ego, with the sole intention of adding meaning to someone else's life.

Because whatever you do there will be a time when you will not be able to do it anymore, and that does not mean that you will have stopped being yourself, since your being is defined by your acts of kindness and compassion. Because if you base your person on what you own, on your knowledge, or on some skill, there will be some moment in your life when you can no longer do it or just not as well as you used to. So, when you're missing what you had or did, you won't be you anymore? Who will you be now? You will run the risk of suffering for everything you do not do or have. Everything was an illusion because you derived your sense of being from something in the material world, which is quite ephemeral in time and space, not solid or secure. It is a projection of your imagination, a dream on which you based your being on something unreal.

Humbleness is not identified with material forms, it is identified with the sense of the value of equality and the true power of the report you make about yourself, of that dimension that is beyond any form of achievement. It goes even beyond your person to become the being. Humbleness is the union of all living beings, in another dimensional plane and not in the projection of the material one.

As we have mentioned, the humble person does not compare, but is aware of the value of others. The internal power that humbleness gives you is not the kind of power like "more than someone else", but rather the power to live life itself flying, but with feet on the ground and including others, being all the same expression of what you accomplished, even if the rest doesn't know. This is how humbleness transcends in yourself. And it does not mean that you have to sacrifice or lose your sense of personal value, rather it becomes a deeper value that penetrates and takes away any achievement of your life by focusing on service.

Also be humble with nature, with flora and fauna. We are all living beings, we are on the same plane. Nature would still work without humans. It would continue to act exactly the same if we did not exist. Never think that humans are above animals or plants, or that they need us. We even need more from them, to survive. We are part of a food chain that would work exactly as well as if we weren't in it. Of all the living beings on the planet, humans are the only ones who disrespect the food chain. And it still works. All living beings are equal.

If you win or lose in your sport, if the ego tempts you into feeling special when you are asked for an interview or a photograph in a magazine, if someone compliments you or makes a comment about something you did or did not get, let it go and travel to a plane without form in which what is most important are your actions towards others. Never base the value of your person based on what you know or achieve, that is completely false and unreal. Your value as a person is in a different world that you must create with your own decision, in which material things like trophies, medals, rankings or championships do not exist.

HOW TO ACHIEVE THE PATH OF HUMBLENESS

1. Separate your mind into several compartments and name each one depending on the activities you do. Just think that if you achieved or did not achieve your goal in one of those compartments, it does not affect any other. It doesn't make you special or not special.
2. Say hello to everyone who goes your way. No matter where you are or who you are with. If the greeting comes with a smile, it is much better.
3. Always congratulate your opponent, whatever the result might have been.

4. Celebrate others' accomplishments just like your own. Feel happy when you hear about other people's bliss.
5. Cheer up someone who feels less because they did not achieve something. Whether a sporting triumph or something that makes them feel disappointed or frustrated.
6. Avoid making fun of someone else at all costs. Not even in your thoughts.
7. Whatever the situation, make those around you feel that we are all the same.
8. Treat nature as if it were your family. Respect it and take care of it. Stay away from its possible risks and get as close as you can to provide care.

CHAPTER 8

Path of Detachment

«If nothing and nobody belongs to you, you will never lose anything or anyone.»

- Ricardo Sala.

Attachment is an emotional mental state of compulsive bonding to a thing or person, created by the false belief that with that thing or person you will be able to be happy.

The Law of Detachment means that in order to be able to enjoy anything in the material physical world (thing or person) you must give up your attachment for it.

It does not mean that you have to give up your desire, your objective, enthusiasm or intention to achieve it, what you give up is attachment and the symbol of its result.

Medals, trophies, prizes and rankings are just symbols. Symbols are ephemeral, transitory. They trigger anxiety to get them, and when you get them, after a certain time, you feel empty because you are putting the symbol above your own being.

Attachment will always be to the symbols, detachment instead, is the relationship you have with your consciousness and enlightenment of being, and that is where the true abundance of happiness and spiritual wealth is. There, where nothing and nobody belongs to you, is the freedom to love. With no attachments to anything.

It doesn't mean that if you have an objective of winning a medal in the Olympics or winning a trophy in a tournament, you won't work for it or that it is not your desire. If you work and train for it as an objective, but you are attached to that result, you will realize that a sort of suffering appears if you do not get it; or if you get it after a while when the result is no longer valid, you will also suffer. If you are attached, you will discover that the journey is not quite satisfactory, much less the big day of your final competition. The ego craves the result, and that is when the road becomes winding and far from the path of the spiritual being.

Attachment to the symbol entails dependence. When you leave it, or it goes away, you think your happiness leaves with the symbol. It is wanting to have that symbol as an inert belonging to your own being. Inseparable. All because you think it belongs to you, but in reality nothing and nobody belongs to you.

If you love a flower in the field, you do not cut it and take it to own it. It would die shortly because it would lose its own essence. If you love a flower you let it be, you enjoy it without having it. You contemplate it, admire and smell its natural perfume, but you leave it in its environment, without attachment. You go and share with it whenever you want, but without thinking that there will never be another flower just as beautiful. In other words, nothing is forever and nothing belongs to you, so avoid that emotional mental state of connection with another person, thing or in the sporting sense, avoid your attachment to the result.

The same happens with people. If you want to own them, they lose their essence. Just as you would lose yours if you belonged to someone else. If nothing and nobody belongs to you, you will never lose anything.

Now imagine that you are a big, strong and leafy tree in the forest. Someone arrives, admires you and thinks that it is possible to take you to live somewhere else. They pull you out with whatever technology they may have and take you with them. In that moment you, the tree, cease to belong to nature and your natural environment to go to another place in which it is not possible for you to live fully. Just like that, as if you were the tree, imagine that the man who takes you away is the medal, the prize, the ranking or the trophy. You stop being you to become a symbol. This is how attachment works in sports and in life. You stop being you to stick to a result that is not even emotionally healthy to live. You want to possess it so much that it will end up consuming you spiritually, since you will be on the material side of the *"want to have"* instead of wanting to *"transcend as being."*

Returning to the mentioned metaphors of the flower and the tree, in both cases they would die, since someone else wishes to possess them, hold them or make them their own. That would be the end result thanks to attachment.

Let it be clear to us that the result or prize is not and will not be forever. It will last, analogically, what the flower already torn from the earth takes to wither outside its environment. That is, very little time.

EVERYTHING IS TEMPORARY

All results are transitory. En passant. You have the opportunity to feel it within yourself, but being aware that this result is only provided for a brief moment and time. Knowing that everything is temporary will make your life more beautiful, since you will know that today you can have it but maybe not tomorrow, and the present will be better valued in your experience. The same goes for your partner, children, family, friends, loved ones and common people. If you actually live thinking that the moments with them are temporary, these will be more intense, since you will not know how much longer you will have the opportunity to enjoy them.

One of the most serious mistakes of Western humanity is to believe that they have time. By believing that you have enough time for everything, you postpone your dreams, plans and actions, because you believe that you can do it, get it or achieve it in some future time. In some *"later."*

For instance, although you actally know that your children are not forever, you act as if they were. You even act as if their life cycles were extended in time and you do not consciously enjoy them to the fullest. You act as if your partner will last a long time with you. You act as if your friends were going to be around you throughout your life. You act as if the job you got will last a long time. You act as if your parents were to cease to exist when they are old, so you stop visiting them frequently when you stop living with them, or stop learning from them every moment. Or the most serious mistake of all: believing that you will stop existing until you are 70 or 80 years old, so if you are 20, 30 or 40 years old you think you still have a lot of time to live. That makes everything happen too fast, or that things even happen without realizing it until they passed, procrastinating dreams.

All the previous examples are serious mistakes that make us numb before things, situations and people with whom we are supposed to be in life. Live knowing that everything, absolutely everything, is temporary, that is where detachment emanates from.

Every time the Zen warrior wields his lightsaber, he does it as if it were the last time he was going to wield it. That way he values the moment. He delivers everything he has in his heart in battle without saving anything, since he knows it could be the last time he can have the chance to hold the lightsaber in his hand. He does the same when he says goodbye to his children every night before sleeping. He hugs and kisses them enjoying the moment to the fullest, since he doesn't know if he will see them again the next morning.

The warrior plans his life with full knowledge that he does not know how long people, situations, opportunities, or calamities will last. He doesn't even know how long he himself will last.

He knows perfectly that neither his saber, nor his horse, nor his partner, nor his children, nor anything, nor anyone belong to him, but that they have been lent to him.

The Zen warrior knows about the Law of Temporality in both painful and pleasant situations. Therefore, in the painful ones he waits patiently for them to pass, facing them with acceptance, adaptability and patience, knowing that at some point in time the pain will pass. Likewise, he enjoys the pleasant situations to the fullest with intensity, joy, passion and love while they last. Always knowing that they have an expiration date, but without knowing it precisely. Simply, nothing is forever.

Like the ego and its fear of acceptance, fear also has its part in attachment. Attachment is afraid that you cannot be happy without the bonded thing or person. It is afraid that there is nothing better in the absence of the symbol or result. It is afraid that it cannot be happy without that person *"that makes me happy."* It is afraid of not achieving its goal. It is afraid that life will not make sense without a certain person, or it fears that the prize cannot be obtained again in case it has previously achieved it. Therefore, it rejoices in the past by making the world see that you were number one at some point. You are attached to that moment because the ego requests so. You want to sustain your importance at the expense of a past result to which, without realizing it, you are completely attached. You put it above your own being.

Nothing or nobody *"makes you"* happy. Happiness is found within each of us and it is a personal decision to experience it.

People generally believe that failure is the opposite of triumph. However, in the spiritual world that is completely false. The opposite of triumph is fear. Everything entailed by the fear of not being able to achieve the desired result.

Detachment can be understood as the lack of hunger and thirst. Think of a dehydrated person who craves liquid or a hungry person who could eat whatever is at hand to satisfy their hunger. That person feels an emptyness that needs to be filled, but no matter how many times they fill it, it will always empty again and they will feel that same lack, for this reason, detachment is that lack of all outside need. To really love, detachment is necessary.

With attachment to the result, you are looking for your happiness in the wrong place. You are looking outside based on a symbol to which culture gave the value you think you need. When you achieve the result and get your prize, it seems to make you happy, but it doesn't. You will find something similar to happiness, as if you find a usurper or imposter, since in a short time you will be insecure of yourself again and you will seek happiness in another result.

How do I identify if I am attached to someone or something? Very simple, if you suffer when they are gone, you are attached. Do not confuse pain with suffering, since they are emotional states of different levels. Pain is natural to the loss of a person. Suffering and the false belief that life for you will not be the same because you cannot be happy in the absence of someone, is an emotional disorder. Likewise, there are people who act the same way when they lose things, they believe that life will not be the same.

Check out your past for a moment. Think of something or someone that you lost and that you thought was irreplaceable. In the moment it went missing, it may have created an emotional state of sadness, anger, wrath, unhappiness or discomfort. Now think about the present and ask yourself: Have I been able to be happy without that person or thing? Have I been happy without the result? If you answered yes, it means you were attached, but not anymore. If your answers where negative, it means that you are still attached. My point is that you do not need to go through the process of grieving and suffering if you are aware that nothing and no one is yours. Therefore, when a person in your life leaves, you will miss them, but never to the point of thinking that life doesn't make sense anymore.

And where did attachment come from? It came from a fiction of happiness created by your culture or your society, or maybe from yourself when you were educated. In the sports world, attachment to the result is one of the most common sources of suffering. The belief that they themselves are the result is so big, that they are lost as persons. It's sad but true. There is too much attachment to the existence of prizes. I recommend living and training to love the sport they practice, detached from their results and achievements. Living every moment intensely and with passion, but without suffering.

To love with detachment is to love without ties. Your heart should not beat for anyone else, but for you. It is nice and beautiful to tell someone that your heart beats for him or her, however, just saying it marks an unconscious state of attachment. Even if it is said metaphorically, it would be medically impossible that without that person in your life your own heart would stop beating, since you would die instantly. It is a very illustrative phrase to define the attachment to another person when referring to love.

To love will never mean suffering, even if we hear it in many places like verses, poems, songs, etc. A person and nature are fully loved with the mental mode in which I can only touch, contemplate, feel and smell without it being mine. To love is not to want, to want is to possess. To love is to be loose, with nothing that binds me to anything or anyone. To love is freedom.

HOW TO ACHIEVE THE PATH OF DETACHMENT

1. Clean your surroundings. Check one drawer where you keep your clothes and clean it by giving away everything you don't really need. Stop thinking that one day you will use it or that it may be useful in the future. Just put it in a box and give it to someone else.
2. Change the way you think. Think that everything is either borrowed or leased. Everything is temporary and does not belong to you. Even if you have a car or house under your name, stop thinking it's yours.
3. Think of three or four loved ones and treat them like the flower in the field.
4. When you get a prize, think it's just a symbol and that it is temporary.

5. Every time you say goodbye to a friend, partner, relative, child or loved one in general, hug them as if it were the last time you are going to be with them. Thus, you will practice detachment and temporality.
6. When you are about to eat any food, think that it is the last time you will eat it, and feel the satisfaction of not owning it and thinking that it is temporary.
7. The next time you train or compete, do it thinking it is the last time you will practice that sport. There will not be a next time. Now, think about how you would carry that out. Now, do so several times, so that you realize that nothing is forever and that no result belongs to you.

CHAPTER 9

Path of Acceptance and Adaptation

«Focus on what there is, not on what you would like there to be. And with what there is, achieve what you intend.»

- Ricardo Sala.

We could define acceptance as the ability to focus emotionally and mentally only with what is in your environment at the present time. Be it a situation, moment or person. Do not focus on what is not there in that moment, or how you would like it to be, focus only on what is there and accept it, naturally and peacefully.

As for adaptation, this is a state that happens simultaneously with acceptance, or immediately after, in which I adapt to what I have just accepted and achieve my intentions at the moment. When I adapt to the moment I feel able to do anything in order to achieve my purpose or objective with my peace left intact. Emotionally controlled. Adaptation is a skill that is achieved through practice and should appear just after accepting the situation.

As with the rest of the spiritual paths, the Path of Acceptance and Adaptation can be applied at all times in sports and life, however, very little practiced by Western athletes in the right way.

A tough athlete may tell me that they can adapt to any situation of the moment and give their best. However, that is only the first yard in the Path of Acceptance. The way to modify the experience through acceptance is what makes the difference in your peace and capacity for action, obtaining the true resources to move forward towards your maximum performance.

When I teach the Path or Law of Acceptance and Adaptation, either individually in a personal coaching, to a whole team or in a workshop open to the public, there is always someone with whom I have the following conversation:

- "Ricardo, excuse me… I can accept the moment and adapt. I have competed in hostile weather and I don't care. I have also competed when injured and I do my best." -someone from the public tells me.

- "Of course, it is a good start. Anyhow, I ask you the following questions: Is there peace inside you? Do you accept the moment as the ideal moment? Do you adapt with emotional control? Do you feel that the moment is perfect for your best performance? Is your ego present in the face of that adversity?" -I answer.

- "No sir, not so much like that. I would obviously like it to be otherwise to do my best."- he replies.

There is where the big difference between accepting and accepting spiritually lies. In the first situation there is a sort of resignation, a state of victim in the face of adversity and the desire to bring the best out of you no matter what. In the second one, there is peace and perfection with the moment. Starting from that mental and emotional state, you begin the action process to achieve your purpose.

Now, not all athletes practice the non-spiritual acceptance just mentioned. In general, acceptance is not practiced in sports nor in life. I have seen hundreds of times when acceptance and adaptation are concepts that do not even figure in the mental resources of a person. Adverse weather conditions for a trail runner, a violent sea for a triathlete or an open water swimmer, a failed execution for a soccer player, tennis player or golfer, a rival's success, pain or fatigue, an unfavorable score, an incorrectly marked ball by an opponent in tennis, the mistake of a referee or umpire in a game, a comment from the public or your opponent, a deficient organization of the event or tournament, etc. are just some examples of circumstances in which athletes completely forget acceptance.

Given the above examples, we can realize that the reactions of athletes are directed to victim roles in which, *if it were otherwise,* they could have gotten better results in terms of performance.

When this role exists, several mental and emotional states can be triggered, such as anger, frustration, discouragement and even giving up the moment. It is commonly known as "giving up the game", "throwing in the towel", "giving it away" or any other acceptation that has to do with giving up your purpose. And why does this happen? Because the moment is not what you considered optimal in your fiction of reality, and for all the excuses that are installed in your mind concerning what is happening, which make you feel that you don't have the ideal elements to achieve your goal.

But what is spiritual acceptance? Spiritual acceptance is vulnerability and surrendering to what exists - and not what you would like there to be or what you would like to have in that moment -. It is putting yourself in a state of immediate action admitting that the moment itself is perfect.

When you accept, there are no inner struggles. You accept that you are *here and now*; there is no need to leave or escape from the moment you have. You surrender to what is in the present, and accepting everything, you eliminate the ego and the importance you want to demonstrate. You have to give up your internal state of war, of emotions that are useless to achieve your goal of being emotionally intelligent and at peace to make accurate decisions.

Now, it is familiar to the mind to accept, but only when conditions are favorable. It is not strange to accept a favorable environment or moment for our emotions. If the referee wrongs in our favor, we accept it and move on. If you have wind in your favor while cycling, you accept it. If you are currently in second place and your opponent who is going first drops out because of an injury and you win, you accept it. If your opponent has a fault, you accept it and keep playing. If your romantic partner treats you very well and has a gesture of kindness, you accept it. If you get promoted at work or you get a raise, you accept it. You see it? You are familiar with acceptance to some extent, since those emotions are of well-being. The issue comes when the moments are adverse, or are not as you would like them to be. There is where the struggle to defend ourselves from what is happening begins, yet, that is where we must begin to experience the spiritual state of acceptance.

In order to travel the Path of Acceptance, it will be necessary to pay attention to what is happening and think calmly that this is what there is in the moment. Then, under that calm that acceptance gives you, start moving to achieve your purpose with what there is and what you have, modifying your own experience for good.

In the state of acceptance you do not judge the moment. There are no "good" or "bad" moments, only moments that, with practice, you will discover are perfect. And I do not mean that the moment is perfect because for some reason it is so to learn from that adversity. I don´t. It is rather to accept the moment because it is so, without looking for the reason why it is so. It is perfect because this is happening and I am 100% focused on what is there, without thinking about what is not there. Creativity and resourcefulness light up to achieve the goal with the tools you have, whether many, few or none. But you will always have your mind and soul that will get you through if you decide so.

All part of being still and peaceful within. Being spiritual is not a way of being, it is about being in touch with your being. Being in peace and in contact with yourself, any event that you qualify as adverse or tragic will be like waves on the surface of the sea, but your being is calm as the bottom of such sea. Outside there may be a hurricane, however, you accept it in the stillness inside you, without regrets or useless emotions. In acceptance, you find all the usefulness at the moment to achieve your purpose. Your interior is in total control of the moment, in an intelligent mental and emotional state, with total acceptance, ready to act or to do nothing that could threaten your objective, depending on the circumstances of the moment.

DOING NOTHING

Sometimes and depending on the situation, doing nothing is the most effective mode of action, nontheless, the least practiced for most of society. Staying still calms emotions and you enter a state of supreme intelligence. Words create inner and outer limits. With silence and nothingness, there are no limits to possibilities.

To accept is to surrender to the external in order to take control over the internal. It is pure vulnerability to be able to see and feel things from another perspective. To accept is to continue participating and continue playing, but without fear of the result that could be due to the adversities of the moment. When adversity or moments which are not ideal for your performance come, the ego will try to be present with a justification that tries to save your person from what will happen.

I will give a small example of the same situation in a sports environment in which Jose -a hypothetical player- will participate, in a sports match of your choice. In the first scenario, there is a Jose who does not practice acceptance, in the second case the same situation will be faced by Jose, but practicing spiritual acceptance:

Halfway through a game, Jose begins to feel an upset stomach. The score is very even and he is down by a very small difference. Jose begins to feel more and more discomfort in his stomach and in his out-of-control internal dialogue he says:

> - "Damn! Why is my stomach hurting? I did not eat anything different! Maybe it was the banana I ate before the game, I

shouldn't have eaten it! I don't know if I can continue playing with this pain that already *made me* lose several points."

- "It is hard enough to beat the guy feeling well 100%, now, even more with a stomachache!" -he kept complaining inside.

Ten minutes after continuing to play with pain, Jose continued with the following internal dialogue:

- "This pain is not going away! I think I'm going to lose today *because of* this stomachache, if I could only not have it, I would be able to win".

His body language was showing complaining and touching his stomach with apparent excess pain. His face was one to notify the public that it hurts a lot and that he is having a bad time.

After another five minutes, Jose drops out of his match and obviously loses it. Leaving the court, he tells his coach, friends and family -

without being asked-, the reason why he lost. Obviously the stomachache. And they tell him:

> - "Don't worry, you would have won easily if it had not been for your upset stomach."

> - "Yes! I would have definitely won had it not been for the stomachache." -Jose concluded.

While it is true the stomachache perhaps influenced the result, it is not less true that his attitude of acceptance of the moment was not adequate. It was not of peace, surrender to pain and action with what there is. While Jose was publicly complaining about his pain, it was the ego who was looking for an excuse to justify that he was going to lose. Also his comment at the end of the game comes from his ego, so he can justify himself and verbally express the reason why he lost. He spent a lot of energy sustaining his pretended importance as an athlete or person.

On the other hand, during his thoughts at the time of the game, Jose focused on the reason why his stomach ached, however, that was not useful at present, since the reason for his pain is completely irrelevant in that moment, that was part of the past. Later on, it rounds up with the thought of: *"I don't know if I can continue playing with this pain that already made me lose several points."* That other comment is in the future and he is attributing the fault of losing to his stomachache. The responsibility to lose was not exclusive of his pain, but also of his attitude towards pain and the total lack of acceptance of the moment by not holding himself accountable for the lack of focus, attention and energy to what was actually there, besides the pain.

Now let's take a look at Jose practicing the Path of Spiritual Acceptance in the same situation:

Jose's stomach hurts during his match and he thinks in a controlled state, without internal conflicts or dramatic emotions. Completely at peace.

> - "Okay, my stomach is aching. I will focus on everything that is useful to me and accept the discomfort as something that is here but does not affect me."

Jose continues playing at the highest level he can have without compromising his health and showing no signs of pain, neither to the opponent nor to the public. Within, there is peace and very little internal dialogue. He decides to remain as still as possible inside, rendered at the moment, but very committed to continue playing with what is there. His energy is strictly focused on what there is to achieve his goal and he continues playing.

During the game and with his upset stomach, Jose constantly looks for options within to continue adapting to the moment. His mind is focused on the game and active to act on what is happening. He is in a state of action with what there is, without dramas or emotional states of feeling victimized. For Jose there is no resistance in his thoughts, and he continues playing for more than forty-five minutes before making the decision to stop playing because of the constant signals that his body sent him with more and more pain.

When he left the game, Jose was above on the scoreboard and winning. His decision was made because he felt he was threatening his body when he felt more and more pain, he realized that a match is not more important than his health. With his educated ego and his being surrendered to the acceptance of the moment, he made his final and definitive decision to drop out and lose the match.

After that, Jose addressed his opponent, shook his hand and congratulated him on his excellent performance and great match. Upon leaving the court, his friends and family asked him why had he dropped out if he was winning. Submerged in peace and tranquility, he replied:

> - "I feel pain in my stomach that did not allow me to continue playing."
> - "Oh, bad luck, had it not been for that reason you would have won!" -a relative replied.

- "I don't know, that didn't happen, besides my opponent played very well." -Jose answered calmly, humbly and without ego.

During the time of the game, Jose never questioned why his stomach ached, he should analyze that at another time, since he understood that that thought was not useful to face the present.

We cannot deny that perhaps the spiritual Jose felt bad for having lost, but such feeling does not feel the same as if it were with ego. Defeat is also accepted in peace. What would victory be like without its sister, defeat? What would life be like without its sister, death? You must accept the moments without resistance, without ego and at peace. Defeat is accepted just as the life, victory or death of another person is accepted. By losing the match, Jose also won. He won in his soul, spirit, humbleness and ego. That has more abundance of well-being than the match itself.

In the case of the Jose who accepted the moment, it could also have happened that he won his match despite his stomachache. I want to clarify that when adversity is accepted incredible and unlimited things are achieved, and that I am not referring to surrendering to the external struggle of an athlete, but to surrendering to what you've got within you that will bring the Zen warrior out of the cave. Whoever practices acceptance never, never, never renounces the struggle to do what is intended with what is there. The one who accepts, adapts immediately in less than a second to what they have and exists. They give the sense of action and perfection to what there is. They become the moment.

Jose's example applies to any situation, and obviously with different outcomes. Acceptance and adaptation are extremely useful with poor execution, in which case it will also have to be accepted. You don't remain in the past or fight thoughts of the type: "I failed!" You accept it and move on, in total peace. You may say it in the moment, but since that past is useless, you let it pass immediately.

With total acceptance and peace, you stop demanding that a moment or person satisfies you. There is where the miracle comes, when you stop demanding the impossible - an ideal state-, everything becomes harmonious to solve the matter. The moment is perfect and you understand it as the simple fact that it is happening, whether it is a favorable or unfavorable situation in your life. Health is accepted just as disease is accepted; a long queue in the bank is accepted as it is accepted when there is no one; an afternoon stuck in a traffic jam is accepted just as it is when traffic is fluent; fatigue during your training is accepted just like it is accepted when you feel very energetic; a rainy afternoon is accepted as is a sunny afternoon; it is accepted that your child leaves to study in another city, just as an injury or accident is accepted. You must accept with peace absolutely everything in life to later adapt to what arrived, directing your energy to what is there, to be able to continue with everything.

Within an apparent chaos you can always find peace within. You are the only one who can make that decision and you must be held accountable for it.

Acceptance is about not arguing with the moment, nor with a person. You need your energy in what is there, do not spend it thinking about what is not there. Stay still for a moment and rethink everything before any change, and take action. Accepting is not resigning to the moment. Resignation is a passive mental state of lack of action. Resigning is not taking responsibility for the moment to act. Acceptance instead is an active state of mind and peaceful search, in which you are 100% accountable for your actions.

When you abandon internal resistance, the circumstances of the moment do not change, what changes is your way of looking at them and facing them, thus improving your experience.

I want to clarify that I am not saying that you should enjoy every moment of acceptance or be happy with a tragical or uncomfortable experience. There is no joy as such when facing a loved one's death, for example. What you have to accept is that pain in order to act. Remember that you also accept favorable moments from your surroundings, such as the fish that accepts the current of the river in favor, or as the birth of a baby is also accepted with bliss. By accepting all that, favorable or seemingly unfavorable, you immediately put yourself into action as a warrior who does not focus his attention on the wound, but rather on continuing to fight externally giving everything he has of his inner part and taking everything there is. What there is will always be enough to give your best.

As we have spoken throughout the present chapter of acceptance of moments and situations, so are people accepted also. You do not wish or demand that they be as you would like them to be. You only accept them and enter a mental state of action so that your experience is harmonious. You focus on what is pleasant and useful about them to achieve the desired peace. Like adverse or favorable moments, people are accepted as they are, since their actions cannot be modified, you have no control over them. They are like the weather or nature, but, you do have control over your acceptance and what happens within you. You have absolute control of your personal experience with them.

Allow people to express themselves just as they are. Only you can calmly allow it because that permission is granted by yourself and it lies inside. Acceptance of the apparently unacceptable is the greatest source of peace that surpasses all understanding.

HOW TO ACHIEVE THE PATH OF ACCEPTANCE

1. Look at everything you have no control over. Observe what is around you when you compete: the weather, your

opponents, your body. Think that you cannot change that, that is what there is. In other words, stop thinking about what you would have liked there to be, and focus 100% on what exists.

2. Now identify how your interior is and modify what you have to modify to achieve your goal with what you accepted in peace from the outside. If you are nervous, accept it and leave only what is useful. Nervousness usually comes with the ego, check the Path of the Ego so that your nervousness decreases or even disappears.

3. Think about what does exist as the rules of this game, those that are in your present moment. This thought should stay away from victim roles, holding you 100% accountable for the actions you are taking or going to take.

4. Look out for every change that happens -in which you have no control- you must accept it without resistance.

5. Keep the ego away in case it appears. Keep it away thinking that there is nothing greater in life than your own being. No competition is bigger than you. What will define you as a person will be your attitude towards what you are living.

6. Never fight against the outside. Don't waste energy fighting it. You will never beat it or modify it. Surrender to it and fight with all the resources you have within.

CHAPTER 10

Path of Happiness

«Of all the questions you have heard the most important one will always be: Are you happy?»

- Ricardo Sala.

Be happy. Perhaps the only obligation that the human being has. So easy to understand, so difficult to practice or achieve. So at hand and so far away when it is not understood or it is confused.

I wanted to leave happiness as the last spiritual path of this book very intentionally. At this point in this journey of peaceful miles, you may have realized that there are not ten spiritual paths of success, but only one path that has all the laws stated in this book. All these laws must be supported by the latter, that of being happy.

I remember that when I first arrived in Nepal, my spiritual masters surprised me a few minutes after arriving at the monastery with a first question:

-"Are you happy?"

To which immediately, in my concept of happiness, I replied:

- "Yes, I am."
- "Very good! And how do you know?" - they replied calmly.
- "Well, because I'm not missing anything. I have loving parents, extraordinary brothers, phenomenal friends. I have done very well in the universities I have been to, I have enough money, with what I live is enough and I even think there might be things in excess. I do what I want, I take care of my body and I feel free. In short, I don't need anything." - I replied.

- "If you don't need anything and you are happy, what are you looking for here?" -asked one of them.

I kept thinking a bit and realized that this type of mental crossroads were what I was looking for to grow. So I replied:

- "I am looking to learn more about myself. I want to look for another way of living and I think I can learn a lot from you here. I seek wisdom for my interior."
- "And how is your interior? Do you feel calm and peaceful?" -they asked.

I paused and began to review my life at a speed that only the mind can do. I remembered that as a child I was at peace in my interior, but when I was older I was not at all because of my frantic life, so full of so many things. To which I replied:

- "No, I don't feel at peace or calm inside."
- "What is keeping you from that?" -they asked.

- "Some fears are keeping me, some guilt for actions I had with other people. Embarrassment or shame with how I treated some of the sentimental partners I previously had, and some other shames with my own parents. Also some wrong decisions I made in the past and mistakes that still affect me. That keeps me from being calm." -I replied.

With a smile on their face, they told me something unforgettable:

- "Here you will learn the concept of happiness, but only you can achieve it, because unfortunately we cannot give you happiness or transfer it to you, still, we can show you the way to it."

And they were absolutely right. I learned the concept of happiness, which was different from what I had. Knowing what happiness is, I could turn to it.

I learned that happiness has nothing to do with being happy or believing that I am missing nothing. People confuse happiness with joy and mention phrases such as: "I feel happy!" instead of "I am happy." By confusing these concepts, it makes them believe that happiness is related to the things and experiences that happen to you. For instance, you are happy if you achieve something or good things happen to you; and you're not happy if you don't achieve something or bad things happen to you.

Spiritual happiness, the one I learned, the one I am currently experiencing and the one I want to explain as simply as possible, is different. It is to have a calm conscience and to be in a state of peaceful serenity within you, knowing that you are on the right path of being well.

Being on the right path is your own decision, which depends on your actions. Precisely, it depends on identifying the decisions you make in your life that may affect your serenity. It is a personal responsibility to build peace from within, without letting the outside diminish it.

You shall keep an eye and be aware of the internal decisions you make based on external life.

Actually, whatever happens is irrelevant. It is only up to you to decide to act with the sole objective of being calm and serene inside. What you do and think yourself is what is really significant.

Never sacrifice your happiness in exchange for having something that you think can define you as a person. Do you think that cyclist Lance Armstrong was happy knowing the way he won so many tours in France? Perhaps now he is, completely freeing himself from when he publicly accepted that he used forbidden substances to win. Today he is at peace and serene, today perhaps he is happy. Before, I doubt it, since said by himself, he had to hide from authorities and set up a whole scene so as not to be discovered. Do you think he lived serene and calm? Therefore, it was irrelevant if he earned millions of dollars in his competitions and sponsorships, if he had a beautiful and caring wife, if he had exceptional children or if everyone prostrated at his feet. He was surely not happy, even if he himself believed at the time that he was, since he sacrificed his happiness for achievements and money. It was as if he lived in hell believing it was heaven.

Other common examples of lack of happiness can be seen every day. What would you feel like if you were involved in deception? Or if you were a politician who committed acts of corruption? Or if you were a debtor who does not comply with their payments? Or if you have a dream that you don't initiate because of fear? Or you have a disease which you don't take care of or attack its cause? Or if you disappoint a friend or your partner? Ask yourself, would you be at peace?

Don't sacrifice anything in exchange for not being happy. In none of the examples mentioned can we say that there is a state of serenity and inner peace as a rule. In all the previous examples there may be moments of joy or pleasure when you obtain something, but the deep sense of peace and inner serenity will not exist. Having pleasure or joy is not necessarily being happy.

To be calm is to know that my decisions are made with the conviction that they are correct according to my values, although I know that the result may turn out to be wrong, I am not mistaken regarding not putting my peace at risk. If you start a business and after a while you have to close because there are losses, don't think that is not being at peace. You may be worried because you have your assets at risk, but things were done correctly and no matter what happens in the environment, there will always be serenity within you, therefore, your happiness will not be threatened.

To be happy is to be calm, whatever happens. It is a cordial relationship between your inner self and the outside. There are no struggles or claims towards what exists outside, nor with what I have or do not have.

My happiness will never depend on an achievement, that would be pleasure and joy. Happiness is walking the path of good. That will bring you genuine well-being. It is a state in which there may be mixed emotions, but with calm.

I want to be sure there is no confusion about it. Being happy has absolutely nothing to do with "having", but with "being". Happiness will never depend on a medal or a trophy, since those symbols will disappear someday. The real struggle is to give life to find happiness, like the Zen warriors of whom I will tell you a beautiful story.

This one afternoon the Zen warrior was letting his horse drink from his village's well. Suddenly a traveler arrived to give the steed he was riding the vital liquid, and while the two supplied their animals, the traveler asked the warrior:

> - "Excuse me, do you know what the shortest way to get to the top of the mountains is? I am looking for something very important for me and I have been told that it is located in the highest mountains of this region."

- "What are you looking for?" -the warrior asked kindly.
- "I seek happiness." -the traveler replied.
- "You are heading to the wrong place friend. Happiness is not located there." - the warrior told him.
- "Impossible! I have gone south, north, east and west. I have gone to the depths of the sea and I am only missing the highest mountains in the world. Besides, I have been told that it is up there where happiness is found and it sounds logical, since it is the only place where I have still to search." -the traveler responded forcefully.
- "You are going to the opposite side." - the Zen warrior insisted.
- "What do you know?! Also, I know I can get anywhere. I am strong, I have the toughest horse in the kingdom and I have a lot of money to reach the end of the world if necessary. I will use all my energy, time, money and possessions to find happiness." -the traveler insisted.

-"Excuse me, good man, but happiness is not found in any of the places you have searched, nor is it at the top of the mountains. Your trip will be useless. Happiness is hidden elsewhere." -the warrior replied.

- "So, do you know where happiness is? I will pay you whatever you ask for if you tell me where it is hidden. Where is it?" -the traveler asked anxiously.

- "Happiness is hidden in a sacred place, where you will have to fight against five dark riders who will not allow you to reach it. When you defeat them, the path will be easier and you will be able reach happiness." -said the warrior.

- "I will fight anyone! Throughout my life I have defeated the strongest, most skillful and daring men in the kingdom! I have also defeated beasts, giants and dragons. I have spent the last years of my life searching for happiness and nobody will stop me from finding it. Who

are those dark riders you mention?" -the traveler asked anxiously for the answer.
- "It doesn't matter who you have defeated throughout your life, friend. These five riders are extremely aggressive and very difficult to beat, yet not impossible. They are called: fear, shame, guilt, drama and ego. You will have to face them with all your weapons and all the spiritual resources you have, since they are fierce and bold riders whose goal is that you never find happiness." -the warrior said calmly.
- "Do I have to defeat them? Can't I get there some other way? Isn't it possible to avoid them to reach happiness?" -the traveler asked.
- "No friend, you can't. You will have to defeat them unavoidably"- replied the warrior.

The traveler took a deep breath and, with a brave look, he told the Zen warrior:

- "Very well, I wish to face them and I will defeat them. But you must first tell me where I should go. What road do I take to reach happiness? Where is happiness and where are the dark riders that I have to defeat? Take me please!" -he exclaimed.

- "Indeed, I know where happiness is and I will tell you, but I cannot take you. Nobody can. It is a personal journey. And what I mentioned before is true, happiness is not found anywhere you have visited and searched, nor is it in the highest mountains. It is closer than you think and closer than most people think it is. There are also no shortcuts or hidden roads. There is only one way which you will have to walk alone."

The warrior paused, looking the traveler in the eyes and facing him, putting one of his hands on his shoulder, the other on the stranger's heart, and he said quietly:

- "Happiness lies hidden inside you and the dark riders you must overcome are also within you."

- "Within me?" -he asked in amazement. "Is happiness within me? And the five riders too? No wonder I would never find it anywhere in the kingdom, in the world or the universe. I have never looked inside me!"

- "I can give you and your horse, food and shelter in my house for the necessary time it takes to overpower the riders. If you wish so, I can even train you spiritually so that you obtain the resources and tools to defeat them." -The warrior proposed.

— "I accept your kind proposal. It is what I have wanted most in my life, to find happiness. I thank you. And, what is your name?" -the traveler asked.

— "I have no name, nationality, or trade. I owe myself to the universe and fight in the service of my BEING and the BEING of humanity, with the goal of achieving my purpose in life, which is to live, give, serve and add meaning and value to the lives of others. You are welcome to my house and you can call me friend." - concluded the Zen warrior.

I believe that being happy is a compulsory commitment. Quitting being happy or never have decided to be so, is sad. It is as letting life just pass by. Without personal significance. It will always be up to you to be happy and to overcome the toxic temptations that life can put in front of you in exchange for not sacrificing or selling your happiness.

Happiness is priceless. It's free and at the same time, not even with all the money in the world can you get it. It is not for sale nor can you buy it from someone else. There is no one that sells it or that can buy yours. It is also not transferable for free. It is such a personal commitment position that it is not possible to transmit it.

Masters or spiritual guides who teach you to find your own happiness cannot do anything to make you happy. For example, I can be by your side when you need me, I can tell you what happiness is, you can feel my happiness, but I can't share it or give it to you. Even though it hurts not to see you happy, I can't make you happy.

What I can do is share tips and tools to be happy. I can help you take a proper spiritual path for you to find happiness, but I can't walk that path for you. I can share and comment on everything in which I've been wrong, I can tell you my mistakes from the past and when I was not happy, so that you don't make some of my mistakes. Your challenge is not being one more person who is happy, your challenge is to be yourself so that you can find your own purpose and live your own happiness.

The outside, external circumstances, the world, its nature, things, and people update us and maybe make us joyful or sad, but they do not define our happiness. You have to leave behind all the characters of yourself that you have created for others. Give up any fictional role that can help you be happy. Instead of using that mask for supposedly finding happiness, bring out the warrior that you are.

In the world of happiness, Zen warriors do not wear masks. To be happy you do not need acceptance from the outside, nevertheless yo do need not to affect any being with your decisions and actions.

On certain occasions, sadness, pain or even anger also manifest when you are happy, but only to pass by. They are only birds of passage that, depending on the circumstance, could appear. In spite of this, feelings of sadness, pain or anger should not alter our serenity and certainty that we are on the path of good. They must not alter our happiness in any way. Like the Zen warrior who loses a partner in battle, he hurts and he is sad, but this does not alter his happiness because he understands the Path of Detachment, acceptance and the true meaning of happiness.

Happiness is also not necessarily being satisfied with everything that happens outside. The universe, the inhabitants of this world, and nature have their own pace and decisions. We are part of that world. We are a species within a genus, for this reason, happiness is something that happens from the skin inside and not outside. Therefore, what happens outside is something that must be completely irrelevant to be happy, as long as you act with compassion, love and kindness. Although hard to believe, practice and spiritual training give you that great ability.

With the permission given to me by having been in both places: in the one of not being happy even sometimes believing that I was, and in the one of being happy, I can tell you I am convinced that the outside has nothing to do with happiness. What is relevant is how you let what happens outside of you influence you, the way you take it or accept it, and even the personal projection you make of the outside.

THE FIVE ENEMIES OF HAPPINESS

Just like the dark riders in the Zen warrior's story, the same five horsemen that must be overcome to find happiness are precisely its enemies, and they are:

1. Fear
2. Shame
3. Guilt
4. Drama
5. Ego

Actually, the enemies of happiness are all those issues that keep you from being yourself.

The *fear* for approval of your actions prevents you from being happy because mentally you are outside and not inside, you stop thinking about yourself to think about society.

The *shame* of having done something in the past that does not allow you to be at peace with yourself. The *shame* of believing that something from your exterior will define you as a person prevents you from being happy.

The feeling of *guilt* of some event or action that does not let you enjoy the present.

The *drama* that tends to exaggerate and project things and circumstances of your life that alter your calm.

The *ego* that makes you wear masks for society and that makes you believe that you owe it.

They are five enemies that you can perfectly defeat. You only need practice and ability to identify them. To be able to eliminate them, you will have to be aware and realize when these enemies appear. If you do not realize that they have seized your being, it will be as if you were asleep or distracted, you will be at their mercy and they will be defeating you without you even noticing that they are doing so.

In the state of happiness there shouldn't be many thoughts, since otherwise, it gets stained or distorted, confusing it with momentary joy or pleasure. It is a state of clarity without so many reasonings. Happiness is a state of abundant peace, which is achieved by making decisions that are within your values, rejuvenating and refreshing you at all times, releasing energy sources from inside you and your body, with the ability to better enjoy your life and sport even with greater physical performance. In this way, without the outside world that affects or threatens your serenity, you will be really living, as you did as a child: fresh, with greater availability to learn, with astonishment of what you see and hear, and with more respect for your inner self. With concerns, those solvable and those that are not solvable, replaceable and those that are not replaceable, they are accepted by your being.

In the state of happiness there are concerns, but they have another tone, another volume, another color, another form. You should not empower any concern to alter your peace, that is, to keep you from being happy. Same with its counterparty, anger. Anger or wrath are your teachers on how to experience calm. Who doesn't notice the difference between anger and peace? It is there where you can compare which state is the one that leads you to happiness.

When you find yourself in moments of pleasure for no reason, accompanied by a state of peaceful serenity, without those moments been caused by personal achievements, having obtained a trophy, medal or recognition, and when these moments last effortlessly even if the external circumstances change, it will then be a sign that you are approaching the state of awakening, the enlightened state of happiness, and there you will have found it.

HOW TO ACHIEVE THE PATH OF HAPPINESS

1. Start with meditation, whether guided or of your own knowledge if you have it. Meditation will help you contact precisely with the place where happiness is found: within. Make yourself familiar with your interior. Meditating is not precisely or necessarily becoming a Zen monk who goes to a mountain to connect with nature and his interior. Meditating is a very simple time to find, once you have

the practice. You can even meditate when you are performing an activity. Start meditating while you are alone. You don't need special clothing or anything other than your body, soul and being. At first, eliminate possible visual or noise pollution, isolating yourself. You can do it during the night while everyone sleeps, in your own bed, lying down, or likewise, way early in the morning when nobody is yet awake at home. After getting yourself acquainted with your interior by meditating regularly, you can start doing it even with noise or while doing something else. The Zen warrior meditates in every action.

2. Practice the Laws or Paths of Self-control and Acceptance in this book. They will help you so that external circumstances do not affect your being and your inner peace.

3. When you make a decision in your life, pay attention to possible outcomes. If you feel that the situation of the

decision will not end well, don't do it. The key is to identify if your decisions will take away serenity and calm in your life. This point is important, since choosing to be calm and peaceful is a decision of your own, made with the intention of achieving an objective that is in your mind, but that shall never affect your inner peace.

4. Never affect someone else with your own decision. It is a rule which will keep you away from happiness if you do not comply with it.

5. Practice the Path of Taming the Ego. It will help you beat most of the enemy riders of happiness.

6. Avoid dramas in your life. Drama is an invention and fiction of yours. Decide to keep it away from you, but without going to the other extreme. Just describe the situation and avoid dramatic interpretations. Drama takes you away from the perception of peace, and that is what you should work on, your inner peace.

7. Start by looking at the world as a movie in which you are the creator and give it the perception you need to be at peace with yourself. Remember that inner peace is synonymous with happiness. Things from the outside happen and are tangible, avoid falling into uncontrolled states, since they will not be created by your world nor created accidentally, but they will be generated by yourself.

Final message from the author:

I wish with all my heart that this book has given you resources so that you can experience your happiness. Live and fight peacefully. Start to travel your own peaceful miles today, or continue relentlessly along that path in case you are already on it.

Namaste.

www.ingramcontent.com/pod-product-compliance
Lightning Source LLC
Chambersburg PA
CBHW071938150726
47999CB00001B/251